Learn Novell® NetWare®
Software in a Day

For Versions 3.11/4.0

Roy B. Brubaker, Jr.

Wordware Publishing, Inc.

Library of Congress Cataloging-In-Publication Data

Brubaker, Roy B.
    Learn Novell NetWare software in a day : for versions 3.11/4.0 /
    by Roy B. Brubaker, Jr.
        p.   cm.
    Includes index.
    ISBN 1-55622-306-4
    1. NetWare (Computer file)   I. Title.
    TK5105.7.B78   1993
    005.7'1369--dc20   92-40054
                                             CIP

Copyright © 1993, Wordware Publishing, Inc.

All Rights Reserved

1506 Capital Avenue
Plano, Texas 75074

No part of this book may be reproduced in any form or by any means
without permission in writing from Wordware Publishing, Inc.

Printed in the United States of America

ISBN 1-55622-306-4
10 9 8 7 6 5 4 3 2 1
9301

PC-DOS is a registered trademark of International Business Machines Corporation.
MS-DOS and Xenix are registered trademarks of Microsoft Corporation.
Novell and NetWare are registered trademarks of Novell Corporation.
Other product names mentioned are used for identification purposes only and may be trademarks
of their respective companies.

All inquiries for volume purchases of this book should be addressed to
Wordware Publishing, Inc., at the above address. Telephone inquiries may be
made by calling:

(214) 423-0090

Contents

Section 1

ABOUT THIS BOOK

INTRODUCTION

This book is organized to teach you how to get your first installation of Novell's NetWare 386 software up and running as quickly as possible. This book has been designed for first time installers, first time LAN administrators, and users who would like a more in-depth knowledge of what it takes to bring a NetWare 386 network to life and keep it alive. For the installation portions, this book assumes that there is not a network already installed. The Novell documentation can be a bit daunting for the novice installer. It is highly recommended that you read this book in its entirety first before you attempt your installation.

Through the use of checklists and "cheat sheets" your installation and configuration is made as fast and trouble free as possible. Please bear in mind that this book should be viewed more as an instructional text than a cookbook. We try to keep the tone of this book as informal and as down to earth as possible. One of the primary reasons for mass confusion regarding network installation is the wanton spraying of acronyms and "insider" phrases.

The focus of this book on NetWare 386 versions 3.11 and 4.0 is due to the wide acceptance of this product and the expansion capabilities of the operating system as your needs grow.

In keeping with getting you up and running as soon as possible, this book will assume a simple NetWare software installation and configuration. The hardware presented as an example in this book consists of the following:

File Server   486 33Mhz ISA bus PC with 16 megabytes of RAM, 1 Ethernet card, 1.44 Megabyte 3½" floppy drive, and a 300 megabyte ESDI hard drive. It also has a VGA video adapter and a multi I/O card containing 1 serial port and 1 parallel port.

ORGANIZATION

This book is organized into sections. Each section guides you through the step-by-step process of bringing your network to life. Following is a list of the sections and their relevance to the task at hand.

Section 1—About This Book: Purpose, organization, and hardware requirements for your network.

Section 2—Novell Concepts: Introduction to the way Novell operates and familiarization of some common terms.

Section 3—Prepare Yourself: Getting your hardware and software prepared and organized.

Section 4—Installing the Server and Workstations: Installing the network software on the server.

Section 5—Installing the Workstations: Preparing the workstations to attach to the network.

Section 6—Setting Up the Users: Adding user information to the operating system and setting up your security.

Section 7—Network Printers: Shared printer installation and maintenance.

Section 8—Setting Up Your Applications: Where and how to set up working network applications.

At the end of the installation sections is a summary of what has transpired. These summaries are by no means meant to replace the text, but to give you a thumbnail sketch of the section.

ABOUT THE DISKETTE INCLUDED

Included with this book is a diskette containing a simple E-Mail and network utility system. It is advisable that you wait until the completion of this book before attempting to install it as there are references to it in several sections of the book. There is also an appendix that describes the installation and operation of the programs.

HARDWARE AND SOFTWARE REQUIREMENTS

Your file server PC should have a processor of at least a 386SX or better with a minimum of four megabytes of RAM and a hard drive. The general rule of thumb on file servers is that more is better. For instance, a 486 processor is much better than a 386 processor; NetWare software can recognize the 486 processor and adjust its operations to suit the processor. The amount of RAM also follows this rule. Four megabytes is minimum, 16 megabytes is much better. NetWare 386 is capable of recognizing and using up to four gigabytes of RAM (4,000 megabytes).

Your workstations should consist of PCs with at least 640K of main memory using DOS version 3.10 or higher. In the interest of simplicity, your workstations should have at least one floppy disk and there should be at least one workstation with a hard drive. We only address those PCs that are running DOS in this book in an effort to keep it simple.

Other equipment on your network should include a tape backup drive in one of the workstations and a UPS (*Uninterruptable Power Supply*) for the file server to be plugged into.

You should have purchased the Novell NetWare 386 operating system. You will also need a legally licensed DOS package for the file server. I recommend either MS-DOS or PC-DOS version 3.30 or version 5.0. MS-DOS and PC-DOS versions 4.0 or 4.01 may be problematic in some cases.

WHAT YOU SHOULD KNOW

You should be familiar with the operation of a DOS based computer, i.e., how to turn it on and off. You should also know the basic DOS commands such as COPY, ERASE (or DEL), FDISK, and FORMAT. You should be familiar with DOS batch files and how they operate. If you need additional information on DOS commands, it is highly suggested that you find a copy of *Illustrated MS/PC-DOS* published by Wordware Publishing, Inc. (consider this an indispensable tool). If you are unable to locate this book, you can contact Wordware Publishing, Inc.

NOTATIONS USED IN THIS BOOK

To help you in using this book, we try to adhere to some simple rules. When we introduce a new phrase that you might want to remember, it is first shown in italics, for example: "The network user information is kept in a group of files called the *Bindery*." DOS and Novell commands are shown in uppercase, for example: USERLIST. We also treat the names of programs and files in uppercase, for example: SERVER.EXE. Instructions regarding keyboard entry have the text that is to be typed in bold and the keys to be pressed listed in brackets (< >), for example: "Type **USERLIST** and press <Enter>."

WARNING!: All components described in this book should be handled and installed strictly according to the specifications and designs of the respective manufacturers. Neither the author nor the publishers can be held responsible for the mishandling of any of the items described or the damages or injuries that may result.

Section 2

NOVELL CONCEPTS

INTRODUCTION

The Novell operating system has evolved over many years to become the premier operating system to link desktop PCs together with each other and to other types of computers both large and small. Over the years, Novell's commitment to the Intel family of computers has helped establish it as the standard by which others are judged. All this power does have a price, however, that being the increasing complexity of getting your network properly installed and maintained. With the power of today's Novell 386, it is possible to install and configure networks ranging from the incredibly simple to the horribly complex. In keeping with the title of this book, we will address the former instead of the latter. (Perhaps later we will publish a book called *Learn Novell NetWare Software in a Year.*)

Following are some terms relating to the Novell operating system you should know before you start.

Volumes - A physical amount of hard disk space that never changes in size. A volume is similar to the root directory on a DOS drive. A major difference is that a Novell volume can span many hard drives. For example, you may have two 300 megabyte hard drives linked to one volume, thereby giving you a 600 megabyte root directory. A volume can consist of up to 32 volume segments. The first volume on a Novell network is always called SYS.

Volume Segment - That portion of a volume that resides on a single hard drive.

Partition - A portion of the hard drive allocated to hold a particular operating system.

Root Directory - The position in the file system where there are no other *"parents"* above it.

FAT (File Allocation Table) - An index of your disk that contains the physical locations of files. This is maintained by the operating system.

Loadable Modules - Programs or drivers that are added to the kernel of the operating system to enhance its capabilities. Loadable modules are known by the acronym NLM (*NetWare Loadable Module*). These modules can be programs such as the installation program or drivers such as you would load to start a network card.

Access Rights - Permissions granted to users to access certain directories, files, or resources on the file server.

Bindery - A group of hidden files on the file server that contain information relating to users, printers, printer configurations, and other network related items.

NIC - An acronym for *Network Interface Card*. This is the piece of hardware you place in your computer to hook in to a cabling system to give you a direct connection to the file server.

MAP - A process by which the user is insulated from long complex directory structures by replacing it with a letter designation.

Now that you have some basic terminology under your belt, we can continue.

DIRECTORY STRUCTURE AND THE NETWORK ENVIRONMENT

Novell directory structures are made to look as much like DOS as possible. For example, look at a typical DOS directory such as:

C:\WP\WORK

If we disassemble the DOS directory, we find the following.

C: Represents the actual DOS *drive* or *partition*.
\WP   Represents the directory underneath the *root directory*.
\WORK   Represents a *subdirectory* beneath the directory of \WP.

The same directory in Novell would be kept track of in the following manner.

SYS:WP\WORK

If we were to disassemble the Novell representation we would find:

SYS: Represents the *volume* upon which the directory resides.

WP   Represents the directory underneath the *root directory* of the *volume*.

\WORK Represents a *subdirectory* beneath the directory of \WP.

As it would be rather tiresome to keep track of a long and complicated subdirectory structure, Novell allows us to *map* or alias a directory name to a drive letter. Mapping is like having a "virtual drive letter"; that is to say, letter K can be used to represent the \WP\WORK directory and letter L can be used to represent the \WP\PLAY directory, but there is no hard drive set up as K or L. You are still on the same volume but instead of using DOS to change directories from WORK to PLAY, you just type L: and press <Enter>.

Note: By default, Novell allows you to have a directory structure 25 levels deep. In a simple example that would give us a directory like F:\1\2\3\4\5\6\7\8\9\10\11\12\13\14\15\16\17\18\19\20\21\22\24\24\25.

If by some set of circumstances 25 is not enough, you can set the *subdirectory tree depth* to 100.

Mapping can be useful in many ways. For example, let's say you have WordPerfect on your file server and Ann, Bruce, and Amy need to have private directories for their work. You could set up WordPerfect to use a mapped drive called F:\WP. Ann could have drive G mapped as \USERS\ANN, Amy would have drive G mapped as \USERS\AMY, and Bruce would have drive G mapped as \USERS\BRUCE. To accomplish this, you would have a *search drive* mapped to the \WP directory and you would run WordPerfect from G: for each user.

Normally, drives A through E are reserved for your local (attached to your PC) floppy and hard drives. Novell does this automatically whether you have drives A through E in your PC or not. You can remap these drive letters to a network directory if you so desire, but you should use the drive letters that aren't actually in use in your PC.

Drives F through H in the example above are letters that have been assigned to network directories. As discussed earlier, these drive letters are impostors, but helpful ones.

Next we encounter what in Novell are called *search drives*. These are directories similar in function to the *paths* used in DOS. In other words, if a command is entered and the program is not in that specific directory, your workstation will look through the search drives and see if it exists in any of those. It will execute the first one it finds.

NETWORK TOPOLOGIES

One of the most crucial elements of a successful network is the choice of the layout of the network. This is referred to as the network *topology*. Simply put, this is the type of network interface cards (NICs) that should be used to connect the file server and workstations together.

The type and configuration of the NICs used on your network should be chosen based on several factors. These factors are speed, cost, and expansion capabilities. The most commonly used network cards for small installations use either the *Ethernet* or *Arcnet* topologies. There are advantages and disadvantages to both. Ethernet provides a fast interface to the file server, however its performance can degrade as the network traffic increases. For a small 5 to 20 node network, this should not present a problem. Arcnet is slower than Ethernet but does not suffer from the same performance degradation as traffic increases.

There are performance tricks you can play with different topologies to increase the total throughput. These primarily consist of installing multiple network cards in the server so that each card serves a segment of the network as opposed to carrying the full load.

INTERFACING HARDWARE WITH NOVELL

Your PC communicates its *requests* (needs for services or files) to the file server via a software and hardware interface. The combination of these two interfaces working in unison are called a *connection*.

THE HARDWARE INTERFACE

The hardware aspect of Novell is theoretically very simple. You place a network card in the file server and use an NLM to activate it. You place a network card in a PC that can talk to the one in the file server.

Hook the two up with the right cable and make sure both are properly activated via software and hardware configuration and you have a network! Sounds easy, doesn't it? Unfortunately, most of the problems associated with firing up a network are related to misconfigured hardware and software for the network interface cards.

Here are some basic terms to review before continuing.

Interrupt - A signal from a hardware device alerting a specific device that it has work to do. Interrupts are commonly abbreviated as *Int*.

I/O Port - The beginning address for an I/O (*Input/Output*) port that an add-in card is configured for. This allows the processor to find a card at a specific area and communicate with it. I/O ports are normally expressed in hexadecimal format, ie: 360h (h denoting hexadecimal). I/O ports are commonly referred to as *port*.

Base Memory Address - A space in memory that some cards may allocate to speed access. This space is often used to buffer or cache the data. No two cards in a PC may be configured for the same memory address. Base memory address is commonly referred to as *memory* or *mem*.

DMA - An acronym for *Direct Memory Access* which is a method for sending and receiving data from a card which can relieve the main processor from having to direct the request to and from memory.

Node - A term used to describe in a generic fashion a PC attached to a file server.

Node Address - A unique number that is assigned to the network card in your PC that identifies each particular workstation on the hardware level. Some topologies, such as Ethernet, assign this number to the network card at the factory. Other topologies, such as Arcnet, allow you to assign this number yourself. There can be no duplicate Node Addresses allowed.

Space does not permit an in-depth description of the various ways to configure your hardware. However, there are some basic rules to make your job easier.

RULE 1:   FOLLOW ALL SAFETY RULES! Make sure equipment is powered off and unplugged before touching it.

RULE 2:   For your first install use the KISS (Keep It Simple Stupid) principle. You can get fancy later.

RULE 3:   Obtain some diagnostic software for your PC. This will allow you to see what memory addresses, I/O ports, and interrupts are already taken before you install your network cards.

RULE 4:   Find a hole and fill it, an unused portion of memory, interrupt, etc. and address your network card to occupy some space in that area.

RULE 5:   Know what is in the PC that you are working on. You will save yourself a lot of heartache if you are familiar with your equipment.

Here are some common memory, port, and interrupt settings you will encounter.

Device	Interrupt	I/O Port	Memory	DMA
Com1	4	3F8-3FF		
Com2	3	2F8-2FF		
LPT1	7	378-37F		
LPT2	5	278-27F		
If LPT3 Exists, then				
LPT1	7	3BC-3BE		
LPT2	5	378-37A		
LPT3		278-27A		
XT Controller	5	320-32F	C800	3
AT Controller	14	1F0-1F8		
		170-177		
Floppy Controller	6	1F0-1F8		2
		3F0-3F7		
Tape Controller	5	280-28F1		3
EGA Video	2	3C0-3CF	A000 or B000 or B800	
VGA Video	2	3C0-3CF	A000	

In order to properly configure your network adapter you must know what not to bang into. To add to the confusion, most cards have a narrow range of I/O ports, memory addresses, and interrupts that they operate at.

You have an Ethernet card to install in a PC with 2 serial ports, 1 parallel port, a bus mouse configured to use interrupt 2, and an ESDI controller. A safe bet would be to use *I/O port* 300h, *interrupt* 5 since there is not a second parallel port in this machine (interrupt 5) and nothing is using I/O port 300h. If we use the same machine and substitute an Arcnet card instead, we would probably use an *I/O port* of 2E0h, *memory address* of D000, and an *interrupt* of 5. These settings represent what you would probably encounter with industry standard network cards.

THE SOFTWARE INTERFACE TO NETWARE 386 3.11 AND 4.0

The software used to activate the hardware installed in your file server and workstations are used in unison to establish and maintain communications. These consist of NLMs for the file server and TSR (*Terminate and Stay Resident*) programs for the workstation. The NLMs are identified by the file extension .LAN and reside on the NetWare installation diskette labeled SYSTEM-2. The workstation programs are contained on a diskette labeled WSGEN. These programs require that the installer configure and create executable programs that would then be copied to the individual workstations. For this reason, it is highly advisable to keep a log of what drivers go in what PCs and how they are configured. These drivers are typically known as IPX.COM and NETX.COM (NETX is used here in a generic context for NET3.COM and NET4.COM; while there is an actual NETX.COM, Novell currently does not ship this with version 3.11 of NetWare software). IPX is always loaded before NETX. Special applications or configurations may cause you to obtain these drivers from sources other than Novell. For example, if you intend to run Microsoft Windows, there are special drivers supplied by Microsoft that you will need for Windows to operate effectively. Since Novell has become the overwhelming standard among operating systems, almost every software publisher supports it. As a rule, every vendor supplies some sort of documentation either on paper or disk on how to run their software under NetWare software.

Novell communication between the file server and the workstations is done via packets. A packet is an addressed chunk of information that consists of several parts. Normally, the first part (the *header*) consists of some information Novell needs to know about what type of packet this is, who sent it, and where it should go. The middle chunk of the packet consists of the action data to be sent down the line. The end portion contains error checking information that allows Novell to verify whether or not all the information was transmitted properly.

NOVELL SECURITY

There are some terms you should know before you delve too far into the security aspects of Novell.

Groups - A definable collection of users who will be using the same applications, printers, etc. For the purposes of administration, it is easier to deal with a collective entity than with individuals.

User - Refers to the individual sitting at his/her computer who needs to access certain directories and printers.

Login Script - A text file that contains a set of commands that are to be executed whenever a user "logs in" to a file server using LOGIN.EXE.

Rights - The privileges allowed for users to access resources on the file server. These rights are *Supervisory, Read, Write, Create, Erase, Modify, File Scan,* and *Access Control.* The *Supervisory* level grants complete access to the directory, including all files and subdirectories. The *Read* level grants users the right to open the files only, or to run a program. The *Write* level grants the right to open and modify existing files. The *Create* level allows a user to create files and subdirectories. The *Erase* level allows a user the right to delete any files in a directory or any of its subdirectories. The *Modify* level allows users to rename directories and subdirectories and change *File Attributes.* The *File Scan* level gives users the rights to see the files in the directory. The *Access Control* level allows a user to modify all of the above rights except *Supervisory.* The user may also temporarily grant more rights to other users.

File Attributes - The characteristics that may be assigned to a file. These attributes include Archive Needed, Copy Inhibit, Delete Inhibit, Execute Only, Hidden, Purge, Read Audit, Read Only, Read Write, Rename Inhibit, Shareable, System, Transactional, and Write Audit.

Directory Attributes - The characteristics that may be assigned to the directory itself. These attributes include Delete Inhibit, Hidden, Purge, Rename Inhibit, and System.

Novell security is arranged in a hierarchal fashion. It is divided into *Group, User*, and special rights. The groups and users created by the installation of Novell should NEVER be deleted! The groups and users created by the installation of Novell should NEVER be deleted! (Got It?)

Groups

When you first install Novell, it creates a group called **Everyone**. This is the group into which every user is placed. The security aspects assigned to this group should grant access to the areas (directories) that every single person on the *LAN* should have access to. The security assigned to a group will also be assigned to all the members of that group.

Users

Users on the network have the rights of the group(s) they belong to and can also have rights beyond that of the group(s). Users can belong to more than one group, and as such, the security privileges from each group are added to the user. For example:

The group **Accounting** has the following rights to the directory called SYS:SSHEETS: Read, File Scan, which Novell would represent as [R F]. User Joe is a member of this group and individually has the additional rights to this directory of Write, Create, Erase, and Modify represented as [**WCEM**]. By adding Joe's group rights to his user rights, Joe's actual rights to the directory would show as Read, File Scan, Write, Create, Erase, and Modify which would be shown as [**RFWCEM**].

A user may also have what is called *Supervisor Equivalence*, which means they have unlimited access to all aspects of the network. When you first install Novell it creates two users, called *Supervisor* and *Guest*. The user called supervisor has unlimited access while the user called guest has the bare minimum access. Supervisor access should be withheld from most users as the potential for damage from well-meaning (or not so well-meaning) users is enormous. Most of your users will fall somewhere in between the two. The groups and users created by the installation of Novell should NEVER be deleted. (Yes again!)

If a user has no access rights to a directory, it will not appear when they type **DIR** at a DOS prompt. If they have limited access, they will see the directory in a normal fashion.

NOVELL INSTALLED DIRECTORIES

The installation of Novell creates four directories and copies programs and data to them. These directories are:

SYSTEM - This is where the server specific NLMs and administrative programs are copied. This area should NEVER be accessed by any of the users except the supervisor.

PUBLIC - This is where a large majority of the Novell utilities are installed that allow the users to manipulate some of their environment. As a general rule, users should only be allowed to search this directory for programs but never create or delete files here.

LOGIN - This is the directory that the users encounter when they first attach to the server. As with the public directory, the users should never be allowed to create or delete files here. The primary program of interest here is called LOGIN.EXE. After successfully running this program, the users really have no other business in this directory (in a simple installation).

MAIL - This directory contains many subdirectories which have the same names as the bindery objects (Users) that they serve. The purpose of these directories is to store certain files that are unique to each user. Because of this, these directories should never be deleted. When you create a new user, the operating system will automatically create a subdirectory under MAIL for that user. The security access to that directory will also be filled in for you. It is very unwise to tinker with this access.

Note: The name of this directory can be misleading in that a person might believe that Novell comes bundled with an *Electronic Mail* package of some sort. This was true long ago (Novell version 2.0a) but no longer.

As stated earlier, the above directories are created upon installation of the operating system. If you want to sleep well at night, resist any urges to change this arrangement.

WARNING

DELETING THE SYSTEM INSTALLED DIRECTORIES AND USERS CAN AND PROBABLY WILL RENDER YOUR SYSTEM TOTALLY INOPERATIVE!

IN CLOSING

When you are in the mood for some heavy reading, you might try reading the book labeled *Concepts* in your Novell NetWare package. It contains an alphabetical listing of all the terms related to almost any aspect of a Novell LAN.

Novell is set up to appear like a big fast hard drive that you've added to a workstation. It just so happens that other people can access your hard drive as well.

Section 3

PREPARE YOURSELF

Before we start, a reminder:

WARNING!: All components described in this book should be handled and installed strictly according to the specifications and designs of the respective manufacturers. Neither the author nor the publishers can be held responsible for the mishandling of any of the items described or the damages or injuries that may result.

The most crucial element of a successful network installation is the preparation and planning before the job is even started. There are many decisions to be made when you decide to install a network. These types of issues can be confusing to the first time installer. The issues that may need to be determined are:

Topology - The type of network interface cards (NICs) that should be used to connect the file server and workstations.

The type and configuration of the NICs used on your network should be chosen based on several factors. These factors (in no particular order) are speed, cost, and expansion capabilities. The most commonly used network cards for small installations use either the *Ethernet* (Figure 1) or *Arcnet* (Figure 2) topologies. There are advantages and disadvantages to both. Ethernet provides a fast interface to the file server; however, its performance can degrade as the network traffic increases. For a small 5 to 20 node network, this should not present a problem. Arcnet is slower than Ethernet but does not suffer from performance degradation as traffic increases.

16

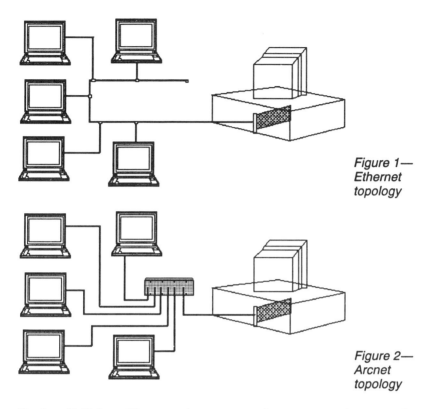

Figure 1—
Ethernet
topology

Figure 2—
Arcnet
topology

Backup Policies - The most important and most expensive part of any network is the data that resides on it. Therefore, it is vital that you have proper procedures and hardware to back your network up. This is one area where saving a few dollars today could cost you literally millions of dollars later on. The most commonly used method of backing up file servers is through the use of tape drives. Under no circumstances should floppy disk backups be considered as the primary backup method.

A good backup policy might consist of daily backups performed on a tape set aside for each day of the week. There should also be a weekly backup performed and that tape should be stored somewhere off site. Safe deposit boxes make nice receptacles for this type of policy.

Applications - Which applications should be made available to what users on the network and which should be kept on local storage.

One of the primary purposes of a network involves sharing applications and data in an easy manner. Practically all software sold commercially today have Novell compatible network versions available. In preparing and planning your network, you must make sure your software is capable of network operation.

Note: While you have the opportunity to check everyone's PC, you should make sure that all the software used is properly licensed and registered. You will sleep much better at night knowing that your LAN and all the software that is used in your office is 100% legal.

You must also decide which method for booting Novell you are going to use. Although Novell is its own operating system, to ease installation and maintenance it requires that you first boot DOS before you start Novell. There are two methods available, *Boot Diskette* and the *Hard Drive* method. The primary advantage of the *Boot Diskette* method is that your Novell operating system executable, SERVER.EXE, can be put in a safe place after starting your server. The primary advantage of the *Hard Drive* method is that the time needed to start your server after it has been shut down is reduced from five minutes to about one minute.

Note: On some of the more exotic hard drive configurations, your only method available is the Boot Diskette method. Some of these configurations refuse to boot DOS.

With the realization that oftentimes the person installing the network software may have no final decision on the makeup of the hardware involved, you, the installer, should at least lobby the powers that be to ensure that all hardware are from a reputable firm. You should ask for and check references from all sources that you use. With the ongoing "Year of the LAN" (going on for at least five years, so far), there has been an explosion of companies who claim to be LAN oriented. Make no mistakes here for you will have to live with the results of hasty or cost-only related decisions.

Not all expert sources are located in towers of steel and glass just as a friendly smile is not a sign of knowledge. In choosing your hardware you may end up using "almost name brand" parts. You should check the track record of these parts as well. Nothing can be more embarrassing than having your network die six months after installation due to marginal hardware.

YOUR WORK AREA

You should have a large desktop area available to you to configure and install the server. This area should have a clean source of power nearby as well as a phone. This phone should have the capability of making long-distance phone calls if needed. You should have a list of all your vendors and their phone numbers near this phone. You should also have a scratch pad and a comfortable chair handy. The top of the table should be covered with an *antistatic* mat that has been set up according to the manufacturer's specifications.

You should have the full set of Novell documentation handy. In the back of this book (Appendix B), you will find worksheets labeled **File Server Worksheet** and **Workstation Configuration Worksheet**. You should make as many copies of these as are necessary and keep them handy. You should have two sets of these copies handy: one that you will fill in with pencil as you progress with your installation and another that you should fill in with ink at the successful conclusion of the installation. This second copy would then become your reference and should be filed in case you need it later on. You should also have a set of tools handy. Office supply stores normally carry a small tool case that is geared towards the needs of the PC user.

You should have **all** the documentation that was supplied to you by the hardware vendors involved. This applies to all the parts that are in your file server, even things such as video cards and I/O cards. These come in handy if a problem arises with hardware conflicts.

THE NOVELL INSTALLER'S CREDO

DON'T PANIC!

As a seasoned installer, I recognize the fact that you can install the same type of server with no problems 99 out of 100 times. For that one time, circumstances may arise that are totally out of your control. I like to blame them on old Russian satellites orbiting overhead, but more realistically, they are normally the result of some subtle changes one or more of the manufacturers may have made to enhance their product. This is not as large a problem today as it used to be back in the good old days, however, it can crop up occasionally. If you are presented with a problem that defies all logic, help is only a phone call away. This is where obtaining all your hardware from a single source really pays off. If you purchased your hardware from a variety of sources, you may experience a phenomenon known as finger pointing. Simply put, this is where Vendor A blames the problem on Vendor B who claims that the problem is really with Vendor A.

PREPARING YOUR FILE SERVER AREA

The area in which your file server will be kept should be the first of your priorities. This area should consist of the following:

Dedicated Power Lines and **Grounded Outlets** - A dedicated power line is one in which there are no other devices of any kind on the same line. The reason for doing so is to prevent any power surges or drains that can occur from the operation of these instruments from affecting the operation of your file server. For the same reasons, a clean and verified ground should be present.

Power Conditioning Equipment - This should consist of an Uninterruptable Power Supply (UPS) with built-in line conditioning. This line conditioning should include spike protection. Even in this modern age of electricity, it is astounding how your local power company can occasionally allow voltage spikes and brownouts to travel the lines. For most applications, a 1200 watt UPS will give you plenty of time to safely handle a power outage.

Static Electricity Protection - In an office environment, static electricity can be a real problem. Understandably, a little extra electricity can make your life real exciting real fast when it comes in contact with delicate electronic equipment. An *antistatic mat* can be obtained from many electronics stores that will fit the bill nicely.

Environment - The area around your file server should be kept cool and in a controlled humidity environment. Most PCs come with manufacturers' recommendations as to the temperature and humidity in which they should be operated. This area should also be as smoke free as possible.

While you are preparing and installing your file server, it is a good idea to plug your UPS into a separate power outlet to ensure that it will be fully charged before your network is ready. A good rule of thumb is to allow for 24 hours of charging.

INSTALLATION OVERVIEW

The first thing you should do, is to find a quiet area to perform your work. This area should have a phone handy, but not a phone that will be in use or ringing constantly. One of the main secrets to successfully installing network software is having a calm, peaceful environment in which to work. If you are unable to find such a spot, you should at least be well rested. Although this may sound irrelevant, a positive attitude is essential to handle any possible problems that may arise.

In order to have as trouble free a network as possible, you should consider some of the following:

1. Purchase a *new* PC to act as the file server. This PC should be from a reputable and reliable supplier. If at all possible, you should consider purchasing as much of the file server components from a single source as possible. You should make sure that the components are all covered by a service policy of some sort.

2. Make sure you have a reliable UPS (*Uninteruptable Power Supply*). Even if you have an old one laying around, I would recommend buying a new one for the file server if at all economically feasible.

3. Have a PC handy with a high density diskette drive of the same type as your file server.

4. Have professionals cable your site. Although this will definitely add to the cost of your network, this is not a place to scrimp. The large majority of problems getting a new network up and running arise from improper or deficient cabling.

To install the network in this book, we make the following assumptions.

1. You have a stable file server candidate that is equipped with quality components.

2. You have had a professional cable company (you've verified their references) install your Ethernet lines from the file server to the workstations.

3. You are using Ethernet cards in the file server and workstations that are compatible with Novell's NE2000 card.

4. You will be booting your file server from a floppy disk, although we will cover preparing your file server to boot from the hard drive.

The installation process is very easy in concept and relatively easy in practice. It consists of preparing the file server hardware and making sure it is operational. After that, you make a boot device (floppy or hard disk) ready for the installation process. You then proceed with the installation process by starting the Novell operating system and running the installation program. Inside this program, you will tell the operating system which hard drive to use and how much, what type of hard drive interface you are using, and what type of network interface card you are using.

After setting up the initial parameters of the installation, you will bring the server completely down and bring it back up again. You will then attach to the server with a workstation and start setting up your user information. At this point, you will also define a network printer and configure that as well.

You will then install some sample applications on the file server and make sure that they operate as they should. After testing your configuration, you will then start letting some of the users on the network one by one.

Users, Groups, and Printers

If you haven't done so already, now is a good time to start thinking about what groups of people are going to work on your LAN. You also will need to think about the nature and location of any printers in the office that you may want to share. In our test installation, we have a dot matrix type printer attached to the file server for everyone's use for spreadsheets and database reports. We also set up a laser printer at a user's workstation to be shared by the word processing department.

User information is normally tailored to a specific individual. Most often, the *User ID* assigned to a person will be his or her first name. In the case where users may have the same first name, you might combine the first name and some of the last name. For example: BILLG and BILLB or MARY_LITTLE and MARY_LAMB.

You should also know what type and level of security you must implement. These levels can consist of the small open type, where no one needs a password to get in the network and no one is worried about others looking at their files. You can have your network set up so that everyone needs a password to get on. You can determine a minimum number of characters they must use for their password and also require them to change their password periodically. You can establish what times during what days of the week the user may access the network. You can also restrict them to logging on from a very specific machine. Only you (and your bosses) can decide how far up the scale you wish to go.

Some Tools and Other Things You Should Acquire

The administrator of your LAN should be armed with the proper tools of the trade to accomplish his/her work with a minimum of fuss and heartache. These tools include a good PC diagnostic program, a subscription to CompuServe (to access Novell's online forums and libraries) and a subscription to *LAN Times* (a periodical that often contains many helpful hints on network administration). You should also purchase some sort of antivirus software. While it may be difficult to convince the "Higher Ups" that these are indeed tools, it will make the LAN administrator's life immeasurably easier.

You will also want to make sure that all your software is properly licensed and registered and that the documentation is within easy reach. You will need to establish guidelines about what people are allowed to copy software on to the server and when. These policies should also include what the users are allowed to copy on to their workstations as well. Although computer viruses are relatively uncommon, they are out there just waiting to pounce on the unsuspecting LAN. It is also a good idea to discourage "sleeping around" on too many BBSs (*Bulletin Board Systems*) with your modem. While most bulletin board systems are well defended and policed against viral invasion, there are some that don't take all the necessary precautions. Once a virus is introduced on a network, it can spread like wildfire.

If you don't have a tape backup unit in one of the workstations that is capable of backing up the network on a single tape, stop right now and go and get one! Get plenty of blank tapes while you are at it. If the unthinkable should happen and your file server croaks, you will be glad that you have a complete set of backup tapes to choose from. In keeping with this, your company should have some sort of "disaster recovery plan" formulated to handle any type of network emergencies.

Depending on the size of your organization and the age of your workstations, you might also want to consider putting them all on a maintenance plan from a reputable provider. This provider should stock any spare parts you might need and should have a local representative for fastest service. Some PC resellers may offer this service to you as part of a "closer" to get you to sign on the dotted line. Just remember that his or her motives and yours aren't always the same. These days, it is reasonable to expect that your PC can be fixed in a few hours or replaced with a temporary loaner while it's out of action.

IN SUMMARY

1. Plan your work and work your plan!

2. Your file server's final resting place should be prepared with a dedicated electrical outlet, a good electrical ground, and a good quality UPS with power conditioning. The area should also fall within the climate conditions specified by your file server's manufacturer.

3. Assemble your file server hardware in a safe, uncluttered area. This area should contain a phone, tools, all hardware documentation, a scratch pad, file server worksheets, and a static free environment.

4. Use only known quality parts in your file server to avoid unnecessary troubles down the road.

5. Plan the makeup of your network groups and resources carefully.

6. Obtain the tools of the trade for the LAN administrator.

7. Implement office procedures to make sure your LAN stays safe and secure.

8. View your LAN as a company wide asset and make sure all your bases are covered in case of a problem.

Section 4

INSTALLING THE SERVER

WARNING!: All components described in this book should be handled and installed strictly according to the specifications and designs of the respective manufacturers. Neither the author nor the publishers can be held responsible for the mishandling of any of the items described or the damages that may result.

PREPARE AND DOCUMENT THE SERVER HARDWARE

As stated earlier in this book, our example file server will consist of the following: a 486 33Mhz ISA (AT-Bus) PC with 16 megabytes of RAM, 1 Ethernet card, 1.44 megabyte 3½" floppy drive, and a 300 megabyte ESDI hard drive. It also has a VGA video adapter and a multi I/O card containing one serial port and one parallel port. Please remember that when we refer to a specific card's settings, we are talking about our test configuration above. If there are generic settings you can try, we will annotate these as such.

Before we start, here are a few terms you should know:

Jumper - This is a pair of copper pins that are connected via a small block of plastic with copper inside. A jumper is understood to be *open* when the pins are not covered by a plug. Jumper switches are normally labeled with the letter "J" and a number in hardware documentation, i.e.: "J-15."

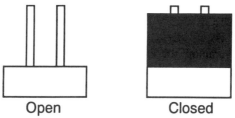

<table>
<tr><td>Open</td><td>Closed</td></tr>
</table>

DIP Switch - A DIP switch is a row of switches in a line which normally have two positions, either on or off. DIP switches are normally labeled with the letters SW, a number, and a switch number in hardware documentation, i.e.: SW-1 (switch 1) 3 (switch position 3).

In front of you, you should have your *File Server Worksheet* (working copy) and tool kit.

WARNING!: Make sure all power is disconnected from every conceivable source before working on any electrical device.

Following the manufacturer's recommended procedures, remove the cover of the PC's chassis. After doing so, you should now be able to see clearly into the PC and begin cataloging all items inside. You do this by using the documentation supplied by the manufacturer. If your manufacturer doesn't provide this information, use the phone NOW and start asking why they did not provide this.

When taking inventory of a PC, it's a good standard procedure to do this looking at the PC from the front and catalog the cards from the power supply (usually on the back right-hand side) and move towards the left.

The first card you encounter as you move to the left should be the hard drive interface card. This card also contains the floppy drive controller. By looking at the documentation and locating the settings on the card, you have determined that this card is set up to use interrupt 14 and a memory address of C800. This is usual for an ESDI card.

At this point, record which of Novell's disk drivers to use. For most applications we can make the following assumptions:

If you have an ISA (AT-Bus) file server and you are using a hard drive that is designated as ESDI or MFM, you should use Novell's ISADISK.DSK driver. If you have a *Microchannel* (MCA) file server with an ESDI controller, you would use Novell's PS2ESDI.DSK driver. If you have a *Microchannel* (MCA) file server with an SCSI controller, you would use Novell's PS2SCSI.DSK driver. If you have a

Microchannel (MCA) file server with a MFM controller, you would use Novell's PS2MFM.DSK driver. If you have an IDE (*Integrated Drive Electronics*) hard drive, you should consult the controller manufacturer's documentation as to which driver to use. Some manufacturers have you use Novell's ISADISK.DSK driver while others may provide drivers of their own. Be aware that some hard drive controllers may or may not belong to one of the groups listed above and the manufacturers will provide their own drivers.

Important Rule: If the manufacturer supplies a Novell driver for the version you are installing, USE IT!

Since your installation is a garden variety ESDI card, use Novell's ISADISK driver. Of course, you write this tidbit of information on your sheet.

The next card you find is the multi I/O card. By looking at the switches and jumpers, you know that LPT1 is set for interrupt 7, port 378. You also know that COM1 is set as interrupt 4, port 3F8.

Now fill in this information on your server worksheet and continue.

Next, we examine the Ethernet card. As luck would have it, it was not installed by the dealer. So, first we locate a free slot on the motherboard. Since this particular card is a clone of Novell's NE2000 card, we know that it needs to be in a 16 bit slot. Motherboard slots on our ISA bus machine are easy to identify because the rows consist of slots of either one or two pieces. The one-piece slots are 8 bit and the two-piece slots are 16 bit. (*Please note that this is what is usually found, your actual slots may vary.*) As you examine the Ethernet card and its documentation, note that it is set for interrupt 4, I/O port 300 (again, this is what is likely to be found). According to the chart of common addresses, you can leave this card as is and it should work just fine. Upon further examination of the documentation, you find that the manufacturer recommends that you use Novell's NE2000 driver that comes with the NetWare software. After you add this information to your worksheet, you can continue. You have located some empty 16 bit slots to the left of the I/O card that your Ethernet card will fit in just nicely. At this point, you should read the Ethernet card manufacturer's installation instructions and comply accordingly.

If you are using Arcnet or some other topology that requires you set the *Node Address* manually, you should do this before you install the card.

A good rule of thumb for manually addressing cards is server network cards should start with the node address of 20 and move upwards from there. Your workstations should start at 50 and move upwards from there. Next you find your Video card and "register" it.

Now that you have accomplished all this work, it is time to put the cover back on and secure it with whatever screws, etc. the manufacturer provides. Being very careful, you can now plug everything back in and make sure there is a generic DOS boot disk in drive A. You may now power your server back on to verify that everything still works OK. If you experience a problem, you should turn everything back off and start over to make sure all the cards are seated properly and you didn't unplug any cables inside accidently.

INSTALLING THE SERVER SOFTWARE

WARNING: If this PC has been used as a workstation, back it up now! Do not proceed until this is done!

Prepare a Start-Up Disk

Now you start your actual installation of the Novell operating system. For this part, use one of the workstations nearby that has a hard drive with some spare room on it. Open the Novell software box and retrieve the two boxes of diskettes. In the brown spacer between the software box and the documentation box, you will find the serialized diskette that contains the "core" of the operating system. This will be in a sealed (stapled and glued) diskette pack. The diskette will be labeled as SYSTEM-1. You need to take a blank high density diskette of the same type as the server's, the following diskettes from the Novell package, SYSTEM-1 and SYSTEM-2, and any special driver diskettes that may have been provided by your hardware manufacturers.

From a workstation with a hard drive, make a directory called SERVER from the root directory:

    MD\SERVER <Enter>

Make that your current directory:

    CD\SERVER <Enter>

Copy the following files from the SYSTEM-1 diskette to your hard drive:

SERVER.EXE
NUT.NLM

Locate the diskette labelled SYSTEM-2 and copy the following files from the SYSTEM-2 diskette:

INSTALL.NLM
VREPAIR.NLM
NMAGENT.NLM

If your network interface card uses drivers supplied from Novell, copy that LAN driver from the SYSTEM-2 diskette. If this is true, the file will have an extension of .LAN, i.e.: NE2000.LAN. In our example, we copy the NE2000.LAN driver.

If your hard drive controller card uses drivers supplied from Novell, copy that driver from the SYSTEM-2 diskette. If this is true, the file will have an extension of .DSK, i.e.: ISADISK.DSK. In our example, we copy the ISADISK.DSK driver.

Your directory should now contain the following:

SERVER.EXE
NUT.NLM
NMAGENT.NLM
INSTALL.NLM
VREPAIR.NLM
NE2000.LAN (or whatever LAN driver you need)
ISADISK.DSK (or whatever disk driver you need)

Get a NEW blank high density floppy of the same type as you will use for the server.

If your workstation is using the same version of DOS that your file server will use, format the floppy with the option to install the DOS operating system. Otherwise, you will need to boot a PC with the proper operating system diskettes and format a diskette using that DOS.

After this is complete, copy the files from the server directory on your hard drive to your floppy.

If you are going to set up your file server to boot from the hard drive instead of a floppy disk, you should copy two additional programs to the floppy.

If your workstation is using the same version of DOS that your file server will use, copy the following from your DOS directory:

FDISK.EXE
FORMAT.COM

If your workstation's version of DOS is different from that which you intend to use for your file server, you need to copy the files from the diskettes that are supplied with your server's DOS.

At this point, you now have a *Server Boot Disk*!

Starting the File Server

Insert your *Server Boot Disk* into the A drive and power on your server and monitor.

Make sure the system date and time are correct in response to the standard DOS prompts.

If you are going to boot Novell from the hard disk, type **FDISK** and press <Enter>.

If this is a PC that was used as a workstation, choose option 4 to display the partition information. Note the partition mapping and write it down on your scratch pad. Using either your particular DOS manuals or your copy of *Illustrated MS/PC-DOS* published by Wordware Publishing, Inc., follow the instructions to delete these partitions. This has been successfully accomplished if the option to display partitions shows that none are present.

To create a boot partition, choose option 1 from the FDISK menu to create a primary DOS partition. You do NOT want to make the entire disk a DOS partition, only about 2 megabytes worth. You must make the primary partition active via option 2 on FDISK (select partition 1 as the one to make active).

After doing the above, choose the view partition option again to view the partition information and make sure it's correct. If it is correct, press the <Escape> key and follow the prompts to reboot your system.

When you have replied to the date and time prompts, you now need to format the hard drive for the DOS operating system. To do so, you need to type the following:

FORMAT C:/S <Enter>

You will be asked if this is what you really want to do. At this point, you might as well reply with "Y" for yes and press <Enter>. If your version of DOS asks for a label, you may just press <Enter> to bypass this. After this step is complete, remove the diskette from the floppy drive and press and hold the <Ctrl> <Alt> keys and press <Del> to reset your server.

Your file server should now boot from the hard drive. If your server fails to boot up from the hard drive, you need to return to the section marked "Starting the File Server" and work back through it to make sure everything was done properly.

At the C:> prompt, copy the contents of the Server Boot Diskette to the hard drive.

After your PC has finished starting up, type the following:

SERVER <Enter>

A few lines below where you pressed <Enter> on the above command, the screen should say something like "Loading......" and stay like that for a few moments.

Note: If you are using the diskette method to start Novell, it may take several minutes before the server program is finished loading.

The screen is now blank and the first question Novell asks is for the name of the server:

```
Novell NetWare v3.11 (20 user) 2/20/91
Processor speed: 915
(Type SPEED at the command prompt for an explanation of the speed
rating)

File server name:
```

You may now type the name that has been decided for your server and press <Enter>. Bear in mind that this name will be converted to all uppercase letters and you are not allowed to use a period (.) or spaces in the name. For our example, you use the name of RN_ADAY for your server. The screen appears as follows:

```
Novell NetWare v3.11 (20 user) 2/20/91
Processor speed: 915
```

```
(Type SPEED at the command prompt for an explanation of the speed
rating)

File server name: RN_ADAY
```

The second question you are asked is for the *internal network number*; this number is significant to the internal workings of the file server. This number must be unique from the other numbers that are used to identify networks in your system. This number must be in hexadecimal using the numbers 0 through 9. Since it is hexadecimal, you may also use the letters A through F. Examples of good hexadecimal numbers are 2001, 2112, A2B, and FEED. A note of caution about using FEED as your internal network number; its use seems to be very popular so if you have other Novell networks that this system may be attached to some day, you may want to resist using it. We use internal network number "2001" to reflect our own personal odyssey. After entering the internal network number, your screen now appears as follows:

```
Novell NetWare v3.11 (20 user) 2/20/91
Processor speed: 915
(Type SPEED at the command prompt for an explanation of the speed
rating)

File server name: RN_ADAY
IPX internal network number: 2001
Total server memory: 15.7 Megabytes

Novell NetWare v3.11 (20 user) 2/20/91
(C) Copyright 1983-1001 Novell Inc.
All Rights Reserved.

Thursday July 30, 1992 10:36:32 am
:
```

At this point, you should be looking at a prompt that looks like a colon (:). The colon prompt is the rough equivalent of the "C:>" prompt in DOS.

Initializing the Hard Drive Adapter

You are now ready to load the driver to activate the hard drives. Remember, in our sample server, we are using the ISADISK driver.

At the colon prompt type the following:

LOAD ISADISK <Enter>

In your installation, you may be prompted for an address and interrupt. You press <Enter> past these prompts if your hard drive controller is set the same as it came from the factory.

At this point, start setting up the hard drive for the Novell area. To do this, we use our first NLM, called INSTALL. At the colon prompt, type

LOAD INSTALL <Enter>

After INSTALL has completed loading, you are presented with a screen such as the following.

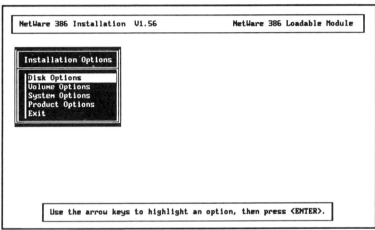

Choose the entry marked **Disk Options** from the main menu.

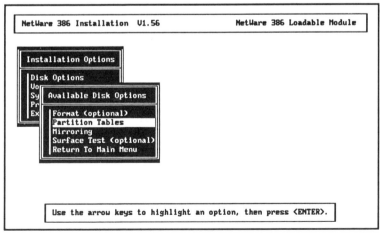

CAUTION: Do NOT choose the option titled "Format (optional)" from the Available Disk Options menu! This option is only to be used at the direction of your hard drive manufacturer.

Choose **Partition Tables** from the options listed on the Available Disk Options menu.

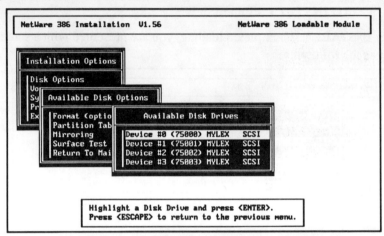

Choose the hard drive to view or modify the partition information on the Available Disk Drives screen. You should then see a screen like:

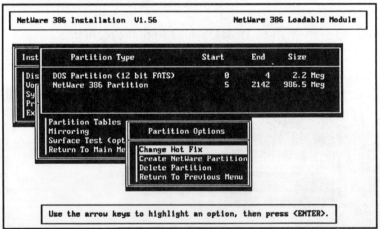

Choose **Create NetWare Partition** from the Partition Options menu.

Choose **Return To Previous Menu** from the Partition Options menu.

Press <Escape> to exit the Available Disk Drives screen.

Choose **Return To Main Menu** from the Available Disk Options menu.

Choose the **Volume Options** entry on the main menu.

You should see a screen like:

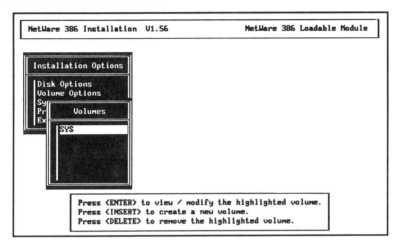

Press <Insert> and you should see a screen similar to the following:

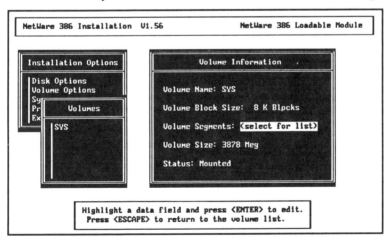

Since this is to be a quick and basically "Default" install, press <Escape> to exit the Volume Information screen. Next, press <Escape> to exit the Volumes screen. You should now be back at the main Installation Options screen.

Choose **System Options** from the main menu and you see the following menu labeled Available System Options.

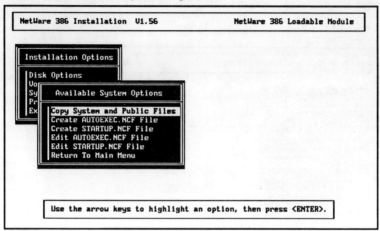

Choose **Copy System and Public Files** from the Available System Options menu.

You are asked if you wish to mount the volume "SYS."

Press <Enter> with the pointer on Yes. Next, you are prompted to insert the following disks in the following order:

SYSTEM-2
SYSTEM-1
SYSTEM-3
UPGRADE
DOSUTIL-1
DOSUTIL-2
DOSUTIL-3
DOSUTIL-4
BACKUP-1
BACKUP-2
PRINT-1
PRINT-2
HELP-1
HELP-2
HELP-3
BTRIEVE

Note: The installation program uses a different method of acceptance than you might be used to; in this program, the <Escape> key is used to signify that the proper diskette is in the drive and that it is OK to continue. To abort this process, you would press the <F7> key.

After you are done, choose **Create STARTUP.NCF File** from the Available System Options menu. You are asked the location of the file to create.

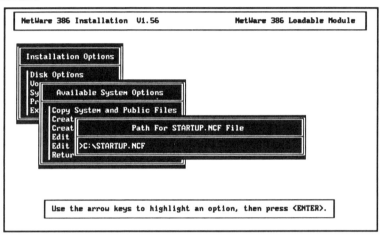

This defaults to the disk where you executed SERVER.EXE from. If you are using the diskette method, put that diskette in the floppy drive and press <Enter>. If you are using the hard drive method, press <Enter> where it displays C:\STARTUP.NCF or A:\STARTUP.NCF.

Press <Escape> and answer **Yes** to the save file question.

Loading the Network Driver

Press and hold the <Alt> key and press <Escape>, then release both to reach the colon prompt. Type the following to load the network driver.

LOAD NE2000 <Enter>

Note: Remember that this is the card type that we are using for our test system.

The driver will load itself and ask you for the I/O port setting of your network interface card.

If the port shown is the same as your card is configured for, you may press <Enter> to accept the answer shown. If this is not the case, type in the I/O port in the manner requested by the driver.

You are next asked to specify what interrupt your card is configured for. Once again, enter the interrupt number for which your card has been set.

If there are no error messages, type the following to establish this board as one that will communicate with DOS workstations via IPX.

> **BIND IPX TO NE2000 NET=99** <Enter>

The network number shown above is treated in the same manner as the *internal network number* described above.

Press <Alt><Escape> to return back to the installation program.

Select **Create AUTOEXEC.NCF File** option from the Available System Options menu.

Press <Escape> and answer "**Yes**" to the question asking you if you want to save what you have done. Press <Escape> out of the installation program until you are asked if you want to "Exit Install."

NOW WE TEST WHAT WE HAVE DONE

At the colon prompt type:

> **DOWN** <Enter>

At this point, wait about ten seconds after the colon prompt returns before you continue. You are doing this to give NetWare the fullest opportunity to write its memory cache back to disk.

To return to DOS, type:

> **EXIT** <Enter>

You should now be at the C or A prompt depending on the start-up method chosen.

If you chose hard disk method, remove the boot disk from the floppy drive. At the C:> or A:> prompt type the following:

> **COPY CON AUTOEXEC.BAT** <Enter>

The cursor drops down a line but the prompt does not return. Next type in the following lines and press <Enter> at the end of each line:

@ECHO OFF
SERVER

Press <F6> or <Ctrl Z> and <Enter> to save the file.

If you are using the hard drive method to boot your server, make sure all diskettes are removed from the floppy drive and power off your server. If you are using the diskette method, insert the Server Boot Diskette you have created and power off the server. After a five or ten minute rest period (Go have a snack, you deserve it!), you should turn your file server back on. This is the final test to ensure that your installation has been completed correctly. It should now go through all the steps necessary and start Novell automatically, leaving you at a colon prompt.

Watch the screen carefully as the operating system goes through all its steps during start-up. In the event that you didn't catch everything as it went by, there are some commands you can try at the colon prompt to verify your system is up and running.

To verify that your network volume initialized and mounted correctly, type the following:

VOLUMES <Enter>

You should see a screen similar this:

```
:volumes
Mounted Volumes      Name Spaces
  SYS               DOS
:
```

To verify that the network interface card driver initialized correctly, type the following:

CONFIG <Enter>

You should see a screen similar to this:

```
:config
File server name: RN_ADAY
IPX internal network number: 00002010

NetWare NE2000 v3.11 (910131)
   Hardware setting: I/O Port 300h to 31Fh, Interrupt 3h
```

```
Node address: 0080C8222684
Frame type: ETHERNET_802.3
No board name defined
LAN protocol: IPX network 00000150
```

If you've made it this far, congratulations are in order. You have just installed one of the most advanced PC network operating systems in the world.

To move around the various screens that the file server uses to monitor its various programs, there are two methods that are used. The first method simply switches screens and is used to view every screen until you reach the one you want. This method uses <Alt><Escape> to cycle the screens. The second method involves using <Ctrl><Escape> to access a list of screens. You then type the number of the screen you wish to view and press <Enter>.

```
Current Screens
    1. System Console
    2. NetWare 386 Print Server
    3. Monitor Screen

Select screen to view:
```

SUMMARY

1. Make sure you are following every possible safety precaution as you build your server.

2. Take an inventory of the items inside your file server and log them on the proper worksheet.

3. Prepare a file server boot disk by formatting a diskette with the proper operating system installed on it (make it bootable).

4. From the SYSTEM-1 Novell diskette, copy SERVER.EXE and NUT.NLM to a special directory on the hard disk of a workstation.

5. From the SYSTEM-2 diskette, copy INSTALL.NLM, VREPAIR .NLM, and NMAGENT.NLM to this directory.

6. Copy the proper hard drive controller driver from either the SYSTEM-2 diskette or a diskette provided by the manufacturer.

7. Copy the proper network interface card driver from either the SYSTEM-2 diskette or a diskette provided by the manufacturer.

8. If you are going to use the hard drive of the file server to boot DOS from, you also need to copy the proper version of FDISK.COM and FORMAT.COM for the operating system you will be using.

9. Copy all the files from this directory to your file server boot disk.

10. Reassemble your file server and boot it with your file server boot disk.

11. If you are going to use the hard drive of the file server to boot DOS from, perform step 12, otherwise proceed to step 13.

12. If you are going to use the hard drive of the file server to boot DOS from, you should now make a small (2 megabyte) DOS partition using FDISK. After rebooting, format the partition with the /S parameter of FORMAT. Copy the contents of the file server boot disk to the C: drive of the server. Reboot the file server from the hard drive and proceed to step 13.

13. At the DOS prompt, type **SERVER** and press <Enter>. Give your server a name and a unique internal network number.

14. Load the hard drive controller driver by executing LOAD *DriverName*. In our example, *DriverName* was ISADISK.

15. Load the INSTALL NLM and choose **Partition Options** from the Disk Options menu. Choose the hard drive from the list and assign all available space left on the drive by choosing **Create NetWare Partition** from the menu. Return to the main installation menu.

16. Press <Enter> on the **Volume Options** selection and the main installation menu and then press <Insert> to make a new volume. Press <Escape> at the Volume Information screen and return to the main installation menu.

17. Choose the **System Options** selection and then choose the **Copy System And Public Files** option from the menu. Feed it all the disks that it asks for.

18. Choose **Create STARTUP.NCF File** from the menu and press <Enter> on the location of STARTUP.NCF. Press <Escape> and answer **Yes** to the Save STARTUP.NCF prompt.

19. Press <Alt><Escape> to return to the colon (**:**) prompt and load the network interface card driver. This is done via the LOAD *NetworkDriver* command. In our example, the *NetworkDriver* was

NE2000. You then respond to the prompts for the configuration of the card.

20. You need to *Bind* IPX as the communications protocol to the card. This is done as follows in our example network:

    BIND IPX TO NE2000 NET=99.

21. Press <Alt><Escape> to return to the installation program and choose **Create AUTOEXEC.NCF File** from the System Options menu. Press <Escape> and answer **Yes** to the save file menu.

22. To properly test your setup, DOWN your server and then EXIT from NetWare. Create an AUTOEXEC.BAT on your boot drive that loads SERVER.EXE automatically.

23. After you power down your server and wait about 10 minutes, power it back up again and make sure everything loads as it is supposed to.

Section 5

INSTALLING THE WORKSTATIONS

OVERVIEW

Probably the least glamorous and most aggravating portion of installing a network involves configuring your workstations to operate on a network. In theory, it sounds very simple. Just slap a network card in, copy a couple of files off a diskette, alter the AUTOEXEC.BAT and CONFIG.SYS files, and *away we go*. Yeah, that's the ticket.

Your job as an installer at this point will also consist of being a states-person (grumpy people who are too busy to leave their PC), a master jigsaw puzzle solver (remembering where all that junk on the top of their PC was supposed to go), and don't forget master advice giver (because 2 months ago someone in accounting had a little problem with their spreadsheet). As you listen to all these irate and/or confused people, remember that you are turning their semi-comfortable world topsy turvy by CHANGING THE WAY THEY WORK. Regardless of the benefits that they will shortly not be able to live without, they will be subconsciously afraid of what is in store for them. You don't have to be a Zen Guru or a faith healer to get by this, just be calm and try to explain the upcoming benefits to the users.

The same basic process used in determining what settings the network card in the file server required also applies here. The major difference between the two is that there are always more variations present in the workstations. For example, a workstation with 1 parallel port, 1 serial port, and an internal modem would give us a net sum of 1 parallel port and 2 serial ports. This is a classic example of making sure you know exactly what is in the PC you intend to connect on the network. The PC architecture has been available for so many years that the number and type of cards that can be installed in your average PC is mind boggling.

Most of your problems in getting a network card to work on a workstation will revolve around finding an interrupt and I/O port that will fit the bill.

Remember, if you are using a topology that requires you to set the *Node Address* of your network card, do this before installing the card in the workstation. The documentation that accompanies your card will have a section on what jumper or DIP switch settings are required to do this. If you are required to set the Node Address manually, it is recommended that your workstation node addresses start at 50 and move upwards. As always, make sure you log this information on your Workstation Configuration Worksheet.

The first PC you will want to attach to the network is yours. It makes for a good practice run as people who tend to get nominated for Novell installer also have a fairly full PC.

There is a worksheet in Novell documentation that you may want to use for your workstation configuration. Oddly enough, it is called the Workstation Configuration Worksheet. You should make a copy for each workstation and staple a printout of that workstation's CONFIG.SYS and AUTOEXEC.BAT for future reference.

PREPARING THE WORKSTATION SOFTWARE

Build IPX.COM

IPX.COM is the TSR Novell uses to activate your network interface card. It is very hardware specific in that it expects to find your card at a specific location in memory and using a certain interrupt. Because of all the possible combinations of addressing and different brands of network adapters, Novell requires that you compile an IPX for each different setting. This is not as bad is it may seem because you are only compiling a 25K program. Each copy of IPX is specific to a particular adapter's hardware settings. The combination of IPX.COM and another TSR called either NET3, NET4, NET5, or NETX are collectively called the *Workstation Shell*. To build the workstation shell, you must first create IPX.COM. The method I recommend most highly (mainly because doing this on a floppy drive is so darned slow) is using the hard drive method.

Here's All You Have to Do

From the "C" prompt on your workstation, type the following:

**CD\
MD\NETWARE
CD\NETWARE
MD WSGEN
CD WSGEN**

Get the WSGEN diskette from your Novell diskette packages.

Your DOS prompt should look like:

C:\NETWARE\WSGEN

Type the following:

XCOPY A:*.* /S <Enter>

After all the files are copied from the WSGEN diskette, type the following:

COPY WSGEN.EXE .. <Enter>

Now type:

CD.. <Enter>

Your current directory should now be C:\NETWARE. You can verify this by typing **CD** and pressing <Enter>.

Next type **WSGEN** and press <Enter>.

The WSGEN program "greets" you with the following screen.

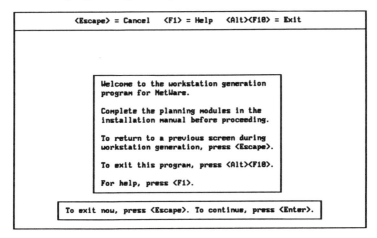

```
   <Escape> = Cancel    <F1> = Help    <Alt><F10> = Exit



         Welcome to the workstation generation
         program for NetWare.

         Complete the planning modules in the
         installation manual before proceeding.

         To return to a previous screen during
         workstation generation, press <Escape>.

         To exit this program, press <Alt><F10>.

         For help, press <F1>.

    To exit now, press <Escape>. To continue, press <Enter>.
```

Press <Enter> and you are presented with a list of standard network interface cards that Novell supports.

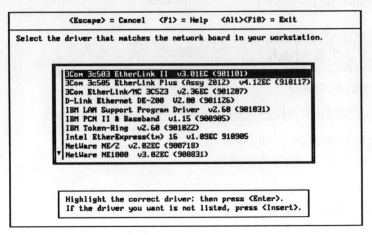

For our example, our cards are not directly listed, however we know them to be compatible with Novell's NE2000 drivers. Using the Down Arrow key, highlight the option labeled as NetWare NE2000 and press <Enter>.

You are next presented with a set of I/O port and interrupt options that Novell supports for this card:

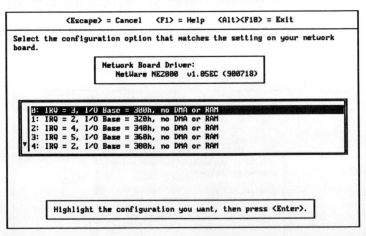

Use the arrow keys to highlight the entry that corresponds to the configuration that you wish to use. Pressing <Enter> on that entry calls the following screen.

If this is the option you wish to generate, press <Enter> on the "Yes" prompt and WSGEN generates the IPX.COM that you need for that card. After the completion of this step, you see the following screen:

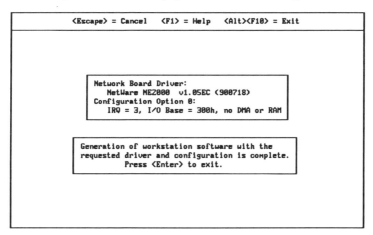

Now change directories to the WSGEN subdirectory by typing:

CD WSGEN <Enter>

You should have in your possession a blank floppy disk labeled on the outside "NE2000 WorkStation Shells." You should make a different subdirectory on this diskette for each of the different configurations you intend to create. I normally call these directories something like 300I3 which I would know stood for I/O base 300, interrupt 3. In the root directory of this floppy, I would copy NET3.COM, NET4.COM, and

NET5.COM (if available). There should be a fresh copy of IPX.COM with today's date and time. You should copy this to the diskette in the proper directory. For example, I would copy the IPX we just made like so: **COPY IPX.COM A:\300I3** <Enter>.

After copying IPX.COM to the diskette, you must return to the NETWARE directory. **Caution: Trying to run WSGEN from the WSGEN subdirectory can confuse the software and will normally require a reboot of your PC to exit.**

You should repeat the WSGEN process for each of the network adapter configurations you will use. If you ever get confused about the configuration of the IPX you just generated, change directories to WSGEN and type **IPX I** <Enter>. This command will ask IPX to show its settings without actually loading it.

The Undiscovered Country

If your workstation candidates have been in operation for any length of time, their AUTOEXEC.BAT and CONFIG.SYS files have evolved into a state where change is both unexpected and unwelcome. There are a few changes that will need to be made. Whatever changes you make to either of these files, make sure the originals are in a safe directory or print them out as a baseline that you can return to if need be. A safe method would be to save them with a text editor as CONFIG.SAV and AUTOEXEC.SAV.

A common problem you will encounter in the CONFIG.SYS file is where someone has set the parameter LASTDRIVE=Z. This is a bad thing in a Novell environment. If the user has some software that needs a LASTDRIVE parameter to operate, see if it can live with the parameter changed to something like LASTDRIVE=E. Another common problem is too many buffers allocated in the buffers line. An example would be BUFFERS=100 or BUFFERS=50. Since the workstation shells altogether require about 50K of memory, every bit you can save is very helpful. Every buffer you allocate in the CONFIG.SYS file takes a chunk of memory. This amount varies from machine to machine. A good place to start would be to set the BUFFERS=20 in the CONFIG.SYS.

If any or all of your workstation processors are 386SX or better, then I would STRONGLY recommend that you purchase an extended memory manager for each of them. Although DOS has gained some memory management in its latter days, it still doesn't come close to the magic that a third-party program can deliver. For example, my usual workstation consists of a 33 megahertz 486 with a 300 megabyte ESDI hard drive, Super VGA, mouse, disk cache, and so on. Using memory managers to load all the TSRs and drivers into *High RAM*, I can have 620K available even after attaching to a Novell network. (That's not bragging, that's what is needed for program development these days.) I have seen some PCs report *740K* of base memory available after a tight optimization.

The FILES statement of your CONFIG.SYS should contain the statement FILES=100. Some applications may require more, so don't be afraid to give it to them.

A sample CONFIG.SYS may look like this:

```
DEVICE=C:\QEMM\MEMM386.SYS R:1 EXT=13312 RAM ROM ST:M
DOS=HIGH
FILES=100
BUFFERS=8
STACKS=9,256
DEVICE=C:\MEMM\LOADHY.SYS /R:1 C:\DOS\ANSI.SYS
```

The above CONFIG.SYS is an example of one using a third-party memory manager. A more generic one might appear like:

```
FILES=100
BUFFERS=20
DEVICE=C:\DOS\ANSI.SYS
```

For more information on what you can and should do with your CONFIG.SYS, you should consult your copy of *Illustrated MS/PC-DOS* published by Wordware Publishing, Inc.

The AUTOEXEC.BAT should be used to load the IPX and NET? drivers.

A sample AUTOEXEC.BAT might look like this:

```
@ECHO OFF
PATH C:\MEMM;C:\DATABASE;C:\DOS;E:\UTILS;C:\WP
C:\MEMM\LOADHY /R:2 C:\DOS\FASTCACH.EXE N H C:12288 S T:9
C:\MEMM\LOADHY /R:2 MOUSE
PROMPT $P$G
LOADHY /R:1 DOSKEY
CD\LAN
LOADHY /R:2 C:\LAN\IPX.COM
LOADHY /R:2 C:\LAN\NETX.COM
```

```
CD\
F:
LOGIN Joe
```

Once again, this example is using a third-party memory manager. The generic version of this would appear as:

```
@ECHO OFF
PATH C:\DATABASE;C:\DOS;E:\UTILS;C:\WP
C:\DOS\FASTCACH.EXE N H C:12288 S T:9
MOUSE
PROMPT $P$G
DOSKEY
CD\LAN
IPX
NETX
CD\
F:
LOGIN Joe
```

THE WORKSTATION HARDWARE

There may be PCs in your environment that have all the motherboard slots filled, thereby leaving you nowhere to place the network adapter. If you encounter this, you should then examine what cards this PC might be able to do without. To avoid all-out war, this should be done with the user's knowledge. If, for instance, this PC has a second I/O card that is not being used (for things like a second parallel port or extra serial ports), that card would be a good candidate for removal. Besides which, those types of cards can steal interrupts or memory addresses that might be put to better use (like for the network).

If you should encounter any serious problems, the manufacturer or supplier of your network adapters is probably just a phone call away. If you need to call them about a problem, make sure you have all the information you can about the nature of the problem *before* you call. This includes all the adapters in the machine as well as the version of DOS, printouts of the AUTOEXEC.BAT and CONFIG.SYS, and so on. If the manufacturer is not able to answer your questions, there should be some local companies who keep their chain-smoking "network gurus" locked away in a room just waiting for your call.

KNOW WHAT YOUR USERS ARE USING

As you deal with each of these PCs, it is a good idea to jot down what applications each person is actually using. You should also verify that you indeed have legal rights to use this package. It may seem harmless and cheaper to run an extra copy of a word processor on somebody's PC, but the potential liabilities involved can be enormous. When the software police come a calling, it's normally because they know something's wrong. Disgruntled employees are their best friend. And by the way, it's also illegal to make unauthorized copies of software. This general rule also applies to any "shareware" programs or utilities you may be using. Registering that nifty little utility ensures that the author can eat and have a place to create even more nifty utilities. End of sermon.

Bringing Them Online

At this point in the installation, it would be sheer folly to bring your users up on the network and leave them there with nothing to do. The recommended practice would be to test the hardware and software combination to make sure that they work and then save the CONFIG.SYS and AUTOEXEC.BAT files to CONFIG.LAN and AUTOEXEC.LAN for use later. Assuming that we are trying this from a PC with a hard drive, a type test session would go like this:

First you make sure that the network cable is properly attached to the network adapter, then you make a directory to store the network drivers.

At the C:\> prompt:

> **MD\LAN** <Enter>
> **CD\LAN** <Enter>

Next copy the correct drivers from the NE2000 WorkStation Shells diskette.

> **COPY A:\NETX.COM** <Enter>   (This workstation is using Windows 3.1.)
>
> **COPY A:\300I3\IPX.COM** <Enter>   (the version of IPX configured for the board in this machine)

Now that we have them where we want them, we can test them.

IPX <Enter>

The screen should show something like:

```
C:\LAN>IPX
Novell IPX/SPX v3.10 (911121)
(C) Copyright 1985, 1991 Novell Inc. All Rights Reserved.

LAN Option: NetWare Ethernet NE2000 V1.03EC (891227)
Hardware Configuration: IRQ = 3, I/O Base = 300h, no DMA or RAM

C:\LAN>
```

Next you see if you can access the file server.

NETX <Enter>   (where **X** is the major version of DOS you are using)

The screen should show something like:

```
C:\LAN>NETX

Novell IPX/SPX v3.10 (911121)
(C) Copyright 1985, 1991 Novell Inc. All Rights Reserved.

LAN Option: NetWare Ethernet NE2000 V1.03EC (891227)
Hardware Configuration: IRQ = 3, I/O Base = 300h, no DMA or RAM

NetWare V3.26 - Workstation Shell (920211)
(C) Copyright 1991 Novell, Inc. All Rights Reserved.

Running on DOS V5.00

Attached to server RN_ADAY
06-05-92  3:45:19 pm
```

If the message is similar to what appears above, then you have connected to the file server. The most important thing to watch for is where it says "Attached to server."

If NETX seems to sit there for a few minutes, then there is a problem with this PC. This can usually be attributed to a problem with the network cable it is attached to. IPX can also be set up for a different interrupt than what the card is actually using. With some network cards, IPX might seem to load successfully even though it is not an exact match for the card. If this occurs, correct either the card settings or IPX.COM before continuing.

If NETX runs quickly (within a few seconds) and reports that "A file server could not be found," then you need to make sure that the network cable is securely (and properly) fastened to the network card.

Because we are such upbeat people, we are going to assume that we got it right the first time. We are now going to attempt to log in to the network as a user to test the connection.

Type the following:

F: <Enter>

LOGIN GUEST <Enter> *Note: LOGIN.EXE is the program Novell provides to identify yourself to the file server.*

You should then see something similar to the following on the screen:

```
G:\LOGIN>LOGIN GUEST
Good afternoon, GUEST.
Drive A:  maps to a local disk.
Drive B:  maps to a local disk.
Drive C:  maps to a local disk.
Drive D:  maps to a local disk.
Drive E:  maps to a local disk.
Drive F: = RN_ADAY\SYS: \
-----
SEARCH1: = Z:. [RN_ADAY\SYS: \PUBLIC]
SEARCH2: = Y:. [RN_ADAY\SYS: \]
SEARCH5: = C:\DOS
```

Let's check the operation of the network by trying a few commands. (Remember, your screens probably will not exactly match the ones shown.)

USERLIST <Enter>   (shows who is logged in to the server)

The screen should show something like:

```
User Information for Server RN_ADAY
Connection User Name      Login Time
---------- -------------- --------------------
    1        FLIP          8-28-1992  7:45 am
    2        SUPERVISOR    8-28-1992  3:40 pm
    3        PRINT_SERVER  8-25-1992 11:30 am
    4      * ROY           8-28-1992 11:34 am
    5        CHRIS         8-28-1992 12:05 am
    6        ANN           8-28-1992  9:12 am
    7        AMY           8-28-1992 11:56 am
    8        BRUCE         8-28-1992 12:39 am
```

WHOAMI <Enter>   (shows who you are logged in as)

```
You are user ROY attached to server RN_ADAY, connection 4.
Server RN_ADAY is running NetWare v3.11 (250 user).
Login time: Friday August 28, 1992 11:34 am
```

SLIST <Enter>   (displays all the servers attached)

```
Known NetWare File Servers          Network  Node Address Status
--------------------------          -------  ------------ ------
RN_ADAY                             [ 2010]  [         1] Default

Total of 1 file servers found
```

CHKVOL <Enter>   (similar to the DOS command
                            CHKDSK in that it shows total drive
                            space and space left over)

```
Statistics for fixed volume RN_ADAY/SYS:

Total volume space:                 3,971,136 K Bytes
Space used by files:                2,335,048 K Bytes
Space in use by deleted files:      1,511,896 K Bytes
Space available from deleted files: 1,508,504 K Bytes
Space remaining on volume:          1,632,696 K Bytes
Space available to ROY:             1,632,696 K Bytes
```

While these are not exactly the showcase NetWare commands, they do allow you to perform some very simple operations on the file server.

If, at any time, you receive a message like "Network Error Sending" or "Network Error Receiving" with a prompt like "Abort Retry Fail," you should reply with an "A" for abort. This problem indicates that there is some sort of communication problem and it should be resolved before you go on. If you are using Arcnet, this could also be a result of duplicate *Node Addresses*.

If all goes as planned, you received the proper answers to your NetWare commands. You can try these commands until you get good and bored. When you are done, you use the following to log out of the file server:

LOGOUT <Enter>   (This program logs the user off of the server but leaves the connection established by IPX and NETX intact.)

After testing a workstation, it is a good idea to reboot it to remove the TSRs from memory until you are ready for this workstation to enter the network for real.

You would then proceed to the next workstation and follow the same steps you just used.

SUMMARY

1. Assess the various options you will need to use your network adapters in your workstations.

2. Be as diplomatic as possible when dealing with the end users.

3. Generate the versions of IPX.COM you will need, using WSGEN installed on a hard drive, and store them in a fashion that makes it easy to remember which one does what.

4. When changing a workstation's AUTOEXEC.BAT and CONFIG .SYS, make sure that there is a safe copy of the originals.

5. Determine the correct hardware settings for the network adapter and install the adapter in accordance with manufacturer's specifications.

6. Test the adapter by temporarily accessing the network and performing a few simple commands.

7. To access the file server, run IPX and then NETx (x = major DOS version 3, 4, or 5). Go to drive F: and type **LOGIN**.

Section 6

SETTING UP THE USERS

OVERVIEW

This section introduces you to the mechanics of configuring your users' environment. This is where the fun really begins since we are assuming that all the nuts and bolts stuff is behind us (except for the printers). Now it's just us and the file server. High noon.

Before getting started, there are some terms that you should be familiar with.

Access Rights - *Permissions* granted to users to access certain directories, files, or resources on the file server.

MAP - A process by which the user is insulated from a long, complex directory structure by replacing it with a letter designation.

Groups - A collection of users who will be using the same applications, printers, etc. For the purposes of administration, it is easier to deal with a collective entity than with individuals.

User - The individual sitting at his/her computer who needs to access certain directories and printers.

Bindery - A group of hidden files on the file server that contain information relating to users, printers, printer configurations, and other network related items.

Bindery Objects - This term refers to any type of entity known to NetWare such as Groups, Users, network printers, and print queues. For higher performance, NetWare assigns each bindery object a hexadecimal number to which it assigns certain properties. These properties vary according to the type. When the user interacts with NetWare, it knows who you are because it has your number. NetWare replaces the numbers with names when the user needs to access these items.

Login Script - A text file that contains a set of commands that are to be executed whenever a user "logs in" to a file server using LOGIN.EXE. There are two levels of login scripts. The first level is the *System Login Script* which is executed by everyone who logs on to the network, and the second level is the *User Login Script* which is assigned to each individual user.

Rights - The privileges allowed for users to access resources on the file server. These rights are *Supervisory, Read, Write, Create, Erase, Modify, File Scan,* and *Access Control.* The *Supervisory* level grants complete access to the directory, including all files and subdirectories. The *Read* level grants users the right to open the files only or to run a program. The *Write* level grants the right to open and modify existing files. The *Create* level allows a user to create files and subdirectories. The *Erase* level allows a user the right to delete any files in a directory or any of its subdirectories. The *Modify* level allows users to rename the directory, change *File Attributes*, and rename subdirectories. The *File Scan* level gives the users the rights to see the files in the directory. The *Access Control* level allows a user to modify all of the above rights except *Supervisory.* The user may also temporarily grant more rights to other users. The term *Trustee Rights* is synonymous with rights.

File Attributes - The characteristics that may be assigned to a file. These attributes include Archive Needed, Copy Inhibit, Delete Inhibit, Execute Only, Hidden, Purge, Read Audit, Read Only, Read Write, Rename Inhibit, Shareable, System, Transactional, and Write Audit.

Directory Attributes - The characteristics that may be assigned to the directory itself. These attributes include Delete Inhibit, Hidden, Purge, Rename Inhibit, and System.

Security Equivalence - The assignment of rights on a file server that is equal to that of another user. Metaphorically speaking, give Jane the same rights as Joe because you already know what rights Joe has.

Supervisor Equivalence - A user that logs in as his or her own unique ID on the network but has been given the same rights as the *Supervisor* User ID.

Queue - A capability to store things that require action. In NetWare, network printers service queues of print jobs. This allows users to continue to submit printouts even while the printer is busy.

Command Line Utility - A program that has no menu interface but relies on there being other words/commands entered at the same time the command is entered.

In addition to the above terms, we will be using some DOS and server based NetWare utilities, as follows:

SYSCON.EXE - A DOS based utility that is used for the configuration of many of the user based characteristics of NetWare.

LOGIN.EXE - A DOS based program that resides in the LOGIN directory of the SYS volume and allows users to identify themselves to the network so they may access network resources. This program reads the user's security settings from the file server's bindery and then executes that particular user's login script.

LOGOUT.EXE - A DOS based program that breaks the workstation-to-file server connection and deletes any network drive mappings that may exist.

SETPASS.EXE - A DOS based utility that allows the end user to modify his or her password. If you have password expiration dates set for a user, this utility is automatically run at login time when their password expires.

MAP.EXE - A DOS based command line utility that can add, delete, or alter your network drive assignment. The MAP program with no parameters entered on the command line shows a list of your current settings.

There are several things you need to accomplish before you start adding the user information. As mentioned in *Section 2 - Prepare Yourself*, you should consider what areas of your office are going to be served by what applications. Those "clusters" of people will be acting as a group as far as we are concerned. We make that assumption on the basis that as a group, these people will be accessing the same basic applications and need access to the same basic directories.

THE LAY OF THE LAN

In the mythical network that we are running, we have several "groups" of people that this network will service. We have a word processing department that does nothing but process correspondence and memos.

We have an accounting department that uses a general ledger package and also does some forecasting in a spreadsheet. The next group we have to accommodate will be the marketing/sales people who also use a spreadsheet in addition to a custom database program to keep track of leads. The last group we need to include is the expert and highly efficient management team that steers this ship through troubled waters. This group needs to be able to access all of the word processing group's programs but not the data. They will be using the spreadsheet program and may want to review the marketing group's database.

On this LAN, we need some sort of *Electronic Mail* (E-Mail) package so that the various people around the office can communicate with each other. (*As luck would have it, there is a simple one included with this book!*) We need some sort of method by which the different departments can share some files. The users each need their own personal directories so that they may store sensitive files in a secure place.

Based on the above information, our groups shape up as follows:

Group Name	Purpose
EVERYONE	Everyone on the LAN
WORD_PROC	Word Processing
ACCOUNTING	Accounting Users
MARKETING	Marketing/Sales People
MANAGEMENT	Management Personnel

Since it is pointless to have groups without people in them, let's get some users.

User Name	Department They Belong To
Amy	Word Processing
Ann	Management
Bill	Marketing
Bruce	Word Processing
Carly	Sales
Chris	Accounting
Desiree	Word Processing
Flip	Word Processing
Hank	Management - Marketing
Roy	Management - LAN Administrator
Tom	Accounting

Now we need to establish what programs we are running and where they are installed. We are displaying the directory names prefaced by the volume name.

Program Name	Purpose	Directory
DBMail	Electronic Mail	SYS:DBMAIL
WP	Word Processing	SYS:WP
321	Spreadsheet	SYS:321
DATABASE	Marketing Database	SYS:DATABASE
ACCTG	Accounting	SYS:ACCTG

We set up most of the programs so that the data are stored in a different directory from the program executables. This is done so that we can control who can access what data in a particular program. We also have a directory called "SHARE" which will serve as a common area.

Program Name	Data Directory
WP	SYS:WP_GRP\DOCS

This directory and its subdirectories are where the word processing department will be saving most of their work.

WP	SYS:ACCT_GRP\DOCS

This is the directory where the accounting group will be saving their documents.

321	SYS:WP_GRP\WKS

This directory and its subdirectories are where the word processing department will be saving most of their spreadsheet work.

321	SYS:ACCT_GRP\WKS

This is the directory where the accounting group will be saving their spreadsheets.

DATABASE	SYS:DATA_DIR

This is the directory where the database files are stored. There is only one directory since the data must be identical for all who access it.

ACCTG	SYS:GL
	SYS:AP
	SYS:AR
	SYS:PAYROLL

Since this program is geared toward a small to midsized company, it gives us no flexibility in where it wants to store its data.

DBMail   SYS:DBMAIL\DATA

This program, like many other E-Mail systems, handles its own directory structures.

Since we want our users to have private directories in which to store their documents and spreadsheets, we also need the following:

User Name	Directories
Amy	SYS:USERS\AMY\DOCS
	SYS:USERS\AMY\WKS
Ann	SYS:USERS\ANN\DOCS
	SYS:USERS\ANN\WKS
Bruce	SYS:USERS\BRUCE\DOCS
	SYS:USERS\BRUCE\WKS

This set of directory requirements can be represented in a tree fashion.

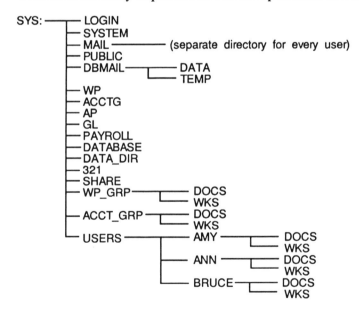

The combination of users, applications, and directories shown can be considered typical for a small-to-midsized network. Based on what you now know, you can begin laying out what rights and access levels you need to grant. In order for you to be able to better relate to the Novell documentation when it refers to rights, we will start representing them the same way they are shown in the manuals. This is done by placing the letter corresponding to the right within braces. For example [RWCEM] would indicate the rights are Read, Write, Create, Erase, and Modify. If you are still having a hard time understanding the *rights mask*, please reread the definition of rights at the start of this section.

First let's examine the group level rights.

Group Name	*Directories*	*Rights* [SRWCEMFA]
EVERYONE	SYS:PUBLIC	[R F]
	SYS:LOGIN	[R F]
	SYS:DBMAIL	[RWCEM]
	SYS:321	[RW MF]
	SYS:WP	[RWC MF]
	SYS:SHARE	[RWCEM]
ACCOUNTING	SYS:ACCTG	[RWCEMF]
	SYS:AP	[RWCEM]
	SYS:AR	[RWCEM]
	SYS:GL	[RWCEM]
	SYS:PAYROLL	[RWCEM]
	SYS:ACCT_GRP	[RWCEM]
MANAGEMENT	SYS:DATABASE	[RWCEMF]
	SYS:DATA_DIR	[RWCEM]
	SYS:MGMT_GRP	[RWCEM]
MARKETING	SYS:DATABASE	[RWCEMF]
	SYS:DATA_DIR	[RWCEM]
	SYS:MRKT_GRP	[RWCEM]
WORD_PROC	SYS:WP_GRP	[RWCEM]

The user level rights are even easier to set up:

User Name	*Directories*	*Rights* [SRWCEMFA]
Amy	SYS:USERS\AMY\DOCS	[RWCEM]
	SYS:USERS\AMY\WKS	[RWCEM]
Ann	SYS:USERS\ANN\DOCS	[RWCEM]
	SYS:USERS\ANN\WKS	[RWCEM]

Bill	SYS:USERS\BILL\DOCS	[RWCEM]
	SYS:USERS\BILL\WKS	[RWCEM]
Bruce	SYS:USERS\BRUCE\DOCS	[RWCEM]
	SYS:USERS\BRUCE\WKS	[RWCEM]

There will be one additional directory for each user that we have not shown in the above list. When you create users in NetWare, the operating system automatically gives them security rights to the subdirectory under MAIL that holds their Login Script. At this point, you might want to study the group and user trustee rights a little more in depth. As you do so, bear a few things in mind. Every user on the network should belong to the group EVERYONE, and on this network there are applications that everyone will need to access. Also remember the group and user rights are additive. If a person is a member of a group, he/she is automatically assigned the trustee rights of the group. The individual user rights are added to all the rights of the group(s) they belong to.

LOGIN SCRIPTS - FRIEND OR FOE?

As explained earlier, login scripts are text files that contain a set of commands that are to be executed whenever a user *logs in* to a file server using LOGIN.EXE. These login scripts can range from the simple "Map some drives and get the heck out of Dodge" philosophy to the "Let's see how many lines we can stuff in this here login script" religion. You could also choose not to have any login script at all and move around the file server by using DOS's change directory command. This last option is not recommended. If this is indeed your first experience with Novell, you will want to subscribe to the first school of thought.

Login scripts can be like a programming language all to themselves much like the DOS batch file language. As an example of this, the following is the default login script that gets executed when a user who has no login script logs on to the network.

```
WRITE "Good %GREETING_TIME, %LOGIN_NAME."
MAP DISPLAY OFF
MAP ERRORS OFF
Rem: Set 1st drive to most appropriate directory.
MAP *1:=SYS:;*1=SYS:%LOGIN_NAME
If "%1"="SUPERVISOR" THEN MAP *1:=SYS:SYSTEM
Rem: Set search drives (S2 machine-OS dependant).
MAP INS S1:=SYS:PUBLIC
```

```
MAP INS S2:=S1:%MACHINE/%OS/%OS_VERSION
Rem: Now display all the current drive settings.
MAP DISPLAY ON
MAP
```

Scary, isn't it. Logging in as the user GUEST produces the following results:

```
Good afternoon, GUEST.

Drive A:  maps to a local disk.
Drive B:  maps to a local disk.
Drive C:  maps to a local disk.
Drive D:  maps to a local disk.
Drive E:  maps to a local disk.
Drive F: = RN_ADAY\SYS: \
     -----
SEARCH1: = Z:. [RN_ADAY\SYS: \PUBLIC]
SEARCH2: = Y:. [RN_ADAY\SYS: \]
SEARCH3: = C:\DOS
```

If we examine the sample login script line by line, we find that its not as bad as it seems. Look at the first line which reads:

WRITE "Good %GREETING_TIME, %LOGIN_NAME."

This line is taking advantage of some information NetWare knows about you and the world you live in. The WRITE statement merely shows something on the screen. The environment information variables that NetWare is constantly keeping track of are preceded by the percent (%) sign. The %GREETING_TIME variable will show the words morning, afternoon, and evening depending on the time of day that you log in. The %LOGIN_NAME variable is simply the name you used when you executed LOGIN.EXE.

The next line, MAP DISPLAY OFF, tells the login process not to show the drive mappings as they are created. After that, is the line

MAP ERRORS OFF

which means simply to bypass displaying errors on the screen if unable to find directories.

The next line is a remark. Remarks in login scripts are handy for documentation in case someone else must maintain the login scripts and needs to know some pertinent information. Remarks must always have, in the leftmost margin, the letters "Rem," a semicolon (;), or an asterisk (*).

The next command illustrates some advanced usage of the MAP statement: MAP *1:=SYS:;*1=SYS:%LOGIN_NAME. This example is ganging two map statements on the same line. The *1 portion of the command means to map the first network drive letter to either be the first available network drive letter (usually F) or the next drive letter after the one specified in your CONFIG.SYS with the LASTDRIVE statement. In this book, we assign the actual drive letters for the purposes of clarity and readability. By using the MAP command as shown above , the result is that the login process will first assign the letter F to the root of the volume (SYS:) and then try to assign letter F to a directory that may or may not be on the server that is named after you. If this second portion is not successful, then your drive letter F remains at the root directory.

The next line illustrates some of the conditional processing that the login process can handle. The line reads:

If "%1"="SUPERVISOR" THEN MAP *1:=SYS:SYSTEM

This line takes a parameter (%1) that LOGIN.EXE is sending and uses it in the login script. If this line were written in English, it would state "If the name of the person logging in was SUPERVISOR then forget what I told you earlier about what the first network drive should be assigned as. Make it map to the SYS:SYSTEM directory." If the login name was not SUPERVISOR, the login process ignores what is after the THEN command.

The next line states that we are going to set up some search drives on the network so that we may run some utilities from other directories.

Rem: Set search drives (S2 machine-OS dependant).

Next we establish some directories on the network to look for programs regardless of where we are. The first line reads:

MAP INS S1:=SYS:PUBLIC

In English, this line reads "into any existing PATH statements you may have already set up in DOS, INSert the first network search directory and make it the SYS:PUBLIC directory."

The next line tries to establish a path to a directory that probably doesn't exist. This command reads:

MAP INS S2:=S1:%MACHINE/%OS/%OS_VERSION

This command makes heavy use of several environment variables. The first of these variables is %MACHINE, which defaults to IBM_PC unless you have specifically changed it. The documentation on how to change this setting is located in the NetWare installation manual in the section about SHELL.CFG settings. The next variable is %OS. The %OS variable refers to the actual type of DOS you are running. The most common of these will be MS-DOS and PC-DOS. The last variable, called %OS_VERSION refers to the actual version of the operating system you are running. Some examples of this would be V3.30, V4.01, and V5.00. The %OS_VERSION always places the letter "V" in front of the DOS version and formats the version as 1 digit for the major version (3,4,5), a period (.) and a two-digit minor version (20, 30, 01, 00). You may have also noted that this line contains forward slashes (/) instead of the usual back slash (\). The NetWare login script will recognize either one, however for reasons of clarity, I only use the back slash (\) to delineate directories for the remainder of this book. You may also notice that this line references S1, which was defined in the line directly above it. The end result of the entire line is that the login process will try to map to a directory called SYS:PUBLIC\IBM_PC\MS-DOS \V5.00 based on the fact that the PC we are using (in our fictional network) is running MS-DOS version 5.0 and we are using an IBM compatible PC.

After viewing another remark, we find the command MAP DISPLAY ON, which reactivates the capability of displaying MAP assignments to the screen.

The final command is simply MAP, which then displays the hard earned results of our login script to the screen.

The end result of all this work is that we have set up some simple drive assignments and search drives on the network upon our logging in, and we are now plopped at a DOS prompt on the network.

In the login scripts that we will be using for our network, we use a few of the items from the sample login script and a few other commands. The login script that we have just dissected is a good example of an *Intermediate* level login script that was mercifully short.

Planning Your Login Scripts

For your own sanity, it is very important that you plan your login scripts on paper before you start plugging away. While you are still new to the concept of login scripts, it is a good idea to work strictly with the user login scripts until you have a very high confidence level in your skills. You should start building your first login script on a few test users until you are sure of what is going on.

CAUTION: Do not test login scripts out on the SUPERVISOR as this can cause you to lose access to your file server as SUPERVISOR.

The best place to start on a login script is to determine the directory needs that the group EVERYONE will have. In our example, the group EVERYONE needs to have access to a core group of applications.

The first thing we write down for our login script is a cordial greeting for all our users. To do so, we borrow a line from the sample login script described earlier.

Our login script looks like this so far:

```
WRITE "Good %GREETING_TIME, %LOGIN_NAME."
```

Next, we establish a drive mapping the E-Mail application which also contains a network menu program to allow our users to choose from the applications they are allowed to run. We set up our first drive to default to this directory. Now your login script is:

```
WRITE "Good %GREETING_TIME, %LOGIN_NAME."

MAP F:=SYS:DBMAIL
```

Next, we assign the drive letters for the next three directories that the group needs to access. Now our login script is starting to shape up.

```
WRITE "Good %GREETING_TIME, %LOGIN_NAME."

MAP F:=SYS:DBMAIL
MAP G:=SYS:321
MAP H:=SYS:WP
MAP I:=SYS:SHARE
```

While we are at it, we set up some search drives that we will need for the proper operation of our applications. We should also get in the habit of commenting our login scripts. In the next login script example we show the configuration of the majority of our drive assignments.

```
Rem: This login script created by Roy on 04/01/92
WRITE "Good %GREETING_TIME, %LOGIN_NAME."

MAP F:=SYS:DBMAIL
MAP G:=SYS:321
```

```
MAP H:=SYS:WP
MAP I:=SYS:SHARE

Rem: Drive letter J will be used for the
Rem: Database application

Rem: Drive letter K will be used for Accounting

Rem: Drive M will be for the group DOCS files
Rem: Drive N will be for the group WKS files

MAP O:=SYS:USERS\%LOGIN_NAME\DOCS
MAP P:=SYS:USERS\%LOGIN_NAME\WKS
MAP INS S1:=SYS:PUBLIC
MAP INS S2:=SYS:321
MAP INS S3:=SYS:WP
Rem: Drive S4 will be used for Database
```

As you have probably already noticed, we made use of the %LOGIN_NAME NetWare environment to set up the individual user's mapping of drive letters O and P to his or her own private directories. We also left ourselves some information that we will need later on.

When a login script is finished executing, it leaves itself in the first network drive letter that is defined. In our case, this means the DBMAIL directory. Since we want the users to enter the E-Mail/Menu package as soon as the login script is finished, we add a new (to us) command type in our login script. This is the type for execution of "external" (non-login script) programs. There are two methods for accomplishing this. The first method is to use a number sign (#) directly in front of a DOS executable. An example of this would be #DMAIL. The other method would be to use an exit statement that would read like EXIT "DMAIL." There are pros and cons to each method. The major downside to the # method is that the login script will remain in memory (and not release that memory for applications) until you exit either the program or the login script. The major upside to this is that you have absolute control over what the user can do and where. The pros and cons of the exit method are the reverse of the # method. The upside is that you have more memory for your applications and the downside is that your control over the user might not be so absolute.

I normally prefer using the exit method and use DOS batch files to minimize my downside. For example, to set up the users so that they access the E-Mail/Menu package from the login script and then log out of the network when they are finished working on the network, I set up a DOS batch file called DBMAILB.BAT and copy it to the SYS:LOGIN directory. The contents of this file are very simple and read like this.

```
@ECHO OFF
DMAIL
LOGOUT
LOGIN
```

The reason for copying this file to the SYS:LOGIN directory is simple. When a user logs out of the network, he has no possible way to access any other directory on the server. But he always has access to the SYS:LOGIN directory to run a batch file. With this in mind, our login script now looks like this:

```
Rem: This login script created by Roy on 04/01/92
WRITE "Good %GREETING_TIME, %LOGIN_NAME."

MAP F:=SYS:DBMAIL
MAP G:=SYS:321
MAP H:=SYS:WP
MAP I:=SYS:SHARE

Rem: Drive letter J will be used for the
Rem: Database application

Rem: Drive letter K will be used for Accounting
Rem: Drive M will be for the group DOCS files
Rem: Drive N will be for the group WKS files

MAP O:=SYS:USERS\%LOGIN_NAME\DOCS
MAP P:=SYS:USERS\%LOGIN_NAME\WKS
MAP S1:=SYS:PUBLIC
MAP S2:=SYS:321
MAP S3:=SYS:WP
Rem: Drive S4 will be used for Database

EXIT "\LOGIN\DBMAILB"
```

Now we toss some conditional processing in our login script so we can have a one-size-fits-all login script. We need to determine whether persons are members of a group. If they are, we map some drive letters to correspond to what they need. Look at our example login script again after some additions and reshuffling and see what's going on.

```
Rem: This login script created by Roy on 04/01/92
Rem: Drive M will be for the group DOCS files
Rem: Drive N will be for the group WKS files
WRITE "Good %GREETING_TIME, %LOGIN_NAME."
MAP F:=SYS:DBMAIL
```

69

```
MAP G:=SYS:321
MAP H:=SYS:WP
MAP I:=SYS:SHARE
MAP O:=SYS:USERS\%LOGIN_NAME\DOCS
MAP P:=SYS:USERS\%LOGIN_NAME\WKS
MAP S1:=SYS:PUBLIC
MAP S2:=SYS:321
MAP S3:=SYS:WP
Rem: Drive letter J will be used for the
Rem: Database application
Rem: Drive S4 will be used for Database
IF MEMBER OF "MANAGEMENT" THEN
MAP J:=SYS:DATA_DIR
MAP M:=SYS:MGMT_GRP\DOCS
MAP N:=SYS:MGMT_GRP\WKS
MAP S4:=SYS:DATABASE
END
IF MEMBER OF "MARKETING" THEN
MAP J:=SYS:DATA_DIR
MAP M:=SYS:MRKT_GRP\DOCS
MAP N:=SYS:MRKT_GRP\WKS
MAP S4:=SYS:DATABASE
END
Rem: Drive letter K will be used for Accounting
Rem: Drive S4 will be used for ACCTG
IF MEMBER OF "ACCOUNTING" THEN
MAP K:=SYS:ACCTG
MAP M:=SYS:ACCT_GRP\DOCS
MAP N:=SYS:ACCT_GRP\WKS
MAP S4:=SYS:ACCTG
END
IF MEMBER OF "WORD_PROC" THEN
MAP M:=SYS:WP_GRP\DOCS
MAP N:=SYS:WP_GRP\WKS
END

EXIT "\LOGIN\DBMAILB"
```

In this new login script, we have made use of the IF..THEN..END capability of the login script. Each IF statement contains a condition that, if it is true, will execute some commands until an END is reached. The IF statements handle the conditional needs of our installation.

As you can see, we made a fairly sophisticated login script rather quickly. We even documented it so that someone later on can see what we were thinking while we created it. If there is a possibility that someone else might be maintaining the login scripts, it is a good idea to leave your name and the date the login script was created and/or modified.

USING SYSCON TO CREATE GROUPS AND USERS

Syscon is the DOS based program used to manage many of the aspects of how your users interact with NetWare. Its features are broken down by major areas. These areas are *Accounting, Group Information, Supervisor Options,* and *User Information.*

The **Accounting** feature can be used to monitor file server usage and charge customers based on the use of file server resources. We will not be activating the accounting feature for this network.

Group Information is used to manage the security and members of clusters of users who have like needs as far as security is concerned.

The **Supervisor Options** area is accessible only by those users who have *Supervisor Equivalence* and is used to manage some of the default values that NetWare assigns to new users.

The **User Information** area is where you create the users' definitions in NetWare and manage their security and drive letter assignments.

To access SYSCON for this section, you need to be logged in to the server as the user SUPERVISOR (*see Section 5 - Installing the Workstations*). If you are already logged on to the file server, you can type **WHOAMI** and press <Enter> to verify that you are logged in as Supervisor. If you are not, type **LOGIN SUPERVISOR** and press <Enter>.

At the F prompt, type **SYSCON** and press <Enter>. You will see a screen similar to the following:

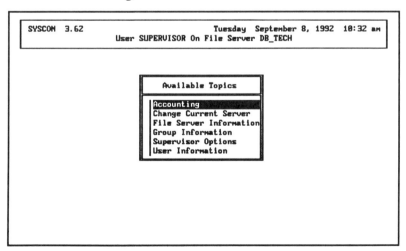

Since we are interested in entering our group and user information, we are not going to use the menu entries called "Accounting," "Change Current Server," or "File Server Information."

Since this is your first glimpse at a Novell DOS based utility, now would be a good time to familiarize yourself with some of the aspects of this interface. To select a menu option, you may either use the arrow keys to highlight the entry you wish, or you may type the name of the option. As you type more of the name of the option, the "selector bar" positions itself on the entry that matches what you have entered so far. If you mistype an entry, your computer beeps at you indicating an error. Online help is available by pressing <F1> at any screen. Pressing <F1> twice produces a list of function key assignments. These key assignments are not specific to the program you are running since they are the standard key assignments that Novell uses in all its menu driven programs.

These keys are:

Function	*Key(s)*	*Description*
ESCAPE	Esc	Back up to the previous level.
EXIT	Alt F10	Exit the program.
BACKSPACE	Backspace	Delete the character to the left of the cursor.
DELETE	Del	Delete an item.
MODIFY	F3	Rename/modify/edit the item.
SELECT	Enter	Accept information entered or select the item.
HELP	F1	Provide on-line help.
MARK	F5	Toggle marking for current item.
CYCLE	Tab	Cycle through menus or screens.
UP	Up arrow	Move up one line.
DOWN	Down arrow	Move down one line.
LEFT	Left arrow	Move left one position.
RIGHT	Right arrow	Move right one position
PAGE UP	PgUp	Move up one page.
PAGE DOWN	PgDn	Move down one page.

Creating Group Information

First we need to create our groups. To do so, place the highlight on **Group Information** and press <Enter>. The following screen appears:

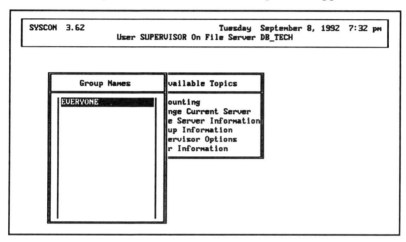

As you can see, the only group defined at this point is the group called Everyone. This is the only group that NetWare will create on installation of the product. This is where we want to create the groups discussed earlier. To add a new group, press <Insert>. The following screen appears:

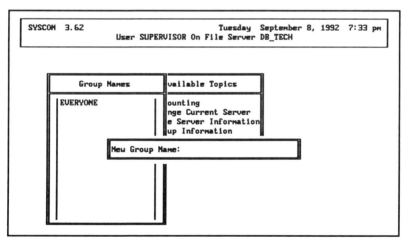

73

The name of the group we wish to add is WORD_PROC for the word processing group. In the box titled **New Group Name:**, type **WORD_PROC** and press <Enter>. After that, we set up some of the group's information. To do this, highlight **WORD_PROC** and press <Enter>. You are then presented with a screen similar to the following:

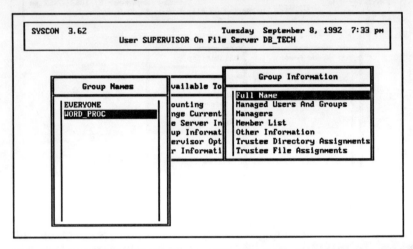

The options on the Group Information menu perform all the functions necessary for the maintenance of the group. The option titled **Full Name** allows you to give a descriptive name to your group. The option titled **Managed Users And Groups** is a method whereby you can grant a group of users the capability to manage some of the security restrictions for that group. The option titled **Managers** is used to designate which users may have access to the security access and alter who is a member of this group. For simplicity's sake, we do not cover **Managed Users And Groups** or **Managers** in this text.

The option titled **Member List** is used to assign users to our groups. The option titled **Trustee Directory Assignments** is used to designate which directories and at what access level the members of this group are allowed. The final option titled **Trustee File Assignments** takes this a step further by designating access on a file-by-file level.

For the purposes of our demonstration, we first choose the option titled **Full Name**. To give our group a full name, place the highlight on that option and press <Enter>. A screen similar to the following appears:

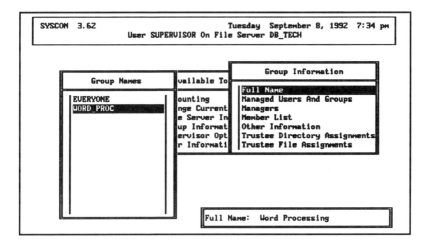

Call our group **The Word Processing Department** by typing this and pressing <Enter>.

Next, proceed to the option titled Trustee Directory Assignments by moving the highlight to the option and pressing <Enter>. The following screen appears:

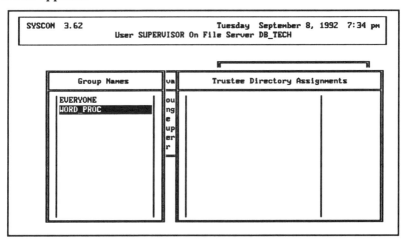

A Trustee Directory Assignment is a directory on the file server that this group can access on some level. There are two methods for filling in this box. The first method is for those who are a little more comfortable with the network directory structure and the way it is addressed. The second method is for those who may not be confident in their knowledge of NetWare directories. We illustrate both methods in an effort to let you decide which method works best for you. To use either method, you must

first press <Insert> to add a new trustee directory assignment. You then
see a dialog box similar to the following:

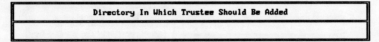

For the users of the first method, you would merely type **SYS:WP_GRP**
and press <Enter>. This represents the name of the volume (SYS) and
the name of the directory that we want this group to access. One of the
many nice things about NetWare is the ability to create directories at this
level. For instance, our directory "WP_GRP" doesn't exist yet, so when
we tell NetWare that we want to give the WORD_PROC group access
to this directory, the following appears:

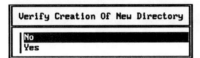

By pressing <Enter> with the
highlight on the "Yes" option, the
directory is created for you.

The alternate method involves a *point* and *pick* scenario in that you are
shown the choices that exist so far. The keys you would use to perform
this method are <Insert> and <Enter>. If you use the directory above as
an example (assuming that the directory SYS:WP_GRP already exists),
you can add the directory as follows:

From the Trustee Directory Assignments list, pressing <Insert> gives you
a screen with the heading Directory In Which Trustee Should Be Added.
Pressing <Insert> again displays a screen like the following:

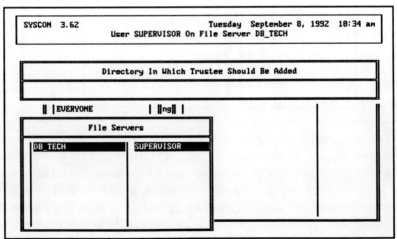

Press <Enter> on the server name and then the next screen with all the volumes for that server appears:

```
 ┌──────────────────────────────────────────────────────────────────────┐
 │ SYSCON  3.62                    Tuesday  September 8, 1992  10:34 am    │
 │                  User SUPERVISOR On File Server DB_TECH                 │
 └──────────────────────────────────────────────────────────────────────┘

   ┌──────────────────────────────────────────────────────────────────┐
   │          Directory In Which Trustee Should Be Added                │
   ├──────────────────────────────────────────────────────────────────┤
   │ DB_TECH/                                                           │
   └──────────────────────────────────────────────────────────────────┘
      ┌──────────────────┐       ┌──────┐
      │ ▌ │ EVERYONE     │       │ ng   │
      │  ┌─────────────┐ │       │ e    │
      │  │  Volumes    │ │       │ up   │
      │  ├─────────────┤ │       │ er   │
      │  │ SYS         │ │       │ r    │
      │  │             │ │       │      │
      │  └─────────────┘ │       └──────┘
      └──────────────────┘
```

Pressing <Enter> on the name of the volume you desire presents you with a list of the directories that are on that volume like so:

Now place your highlight over the directory you want to add to your "dynamic" list at the top of the screen. If you wish to move further down the directory tree, continue using <Enter> to build the directory name. When you have the directory name you want to add (the whole

directory name appears properly in the box titled Directory In Which Trustee Should Be Added), pressing <Escape> returns you to the **Directory In Which...** box. Press <Enter> at this point and you have your directory name inserted into the box titled Trustee Directory Assignments.

The primary benefits of the first method over the second is speed of entry and the ease in which directories can be created. The second method's main benefit is ease of use. By using the second method, only the directories that currently exist are shown in the "list boxes."

Now that you have added a trustee directory assignment, you need to alter the *trustee rights* for this group and directory. Do this by placing the highlight over the directory you wish to alter and pressing <Enter>. You are greeted with a screen similar to the following:

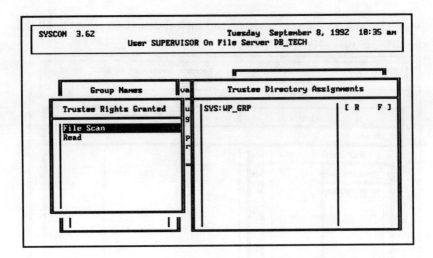

When you add a directory to the Trustee Directory Assignments, NetWare defaults the trustee rights to "File Scan" and "Read." As you may recall from our example, you need to add some extra trustee rights for this directory. Do this by pressing <Insert> on the **Trustee Rights Granted** screen. This calls a screen similar to the following:

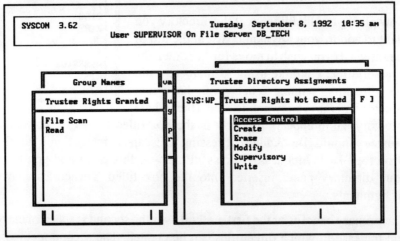

The list marked Trustee Rights Not Granted indicates the directory attributes that do not apply to this directory. To add one of the attributes to the directory rights, highlight the one desired and press <Enter>. If you have an attribute that you wish to remove, highlight the offender and press <Delete>. In our example, we wanted to have the attributes of Read,

78

Write, Create, Erase, and Modify. By using the <Insert> and <Delete> key combinations, we end up with a list that looks like:

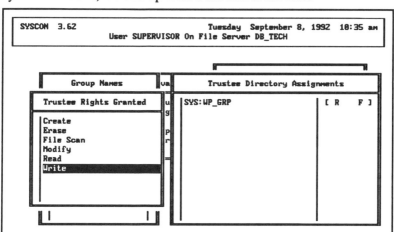

When you are finished altering the trustee directory assignments, you may press <Escape> to save them.

At this point, we probably want to have a break and get ourselves a can of soda to settle ourselves down. After all, we just created a new network entity which should live a long and productive life with a minimum of care and feeding.

The basic procedures you went through to add a group and its directory assignments can be viewed (through squinted eyes) as the basic methods you would use to alter any of NetWare's objects. For example, the keyboard interface used throughout all of NetWare's menu driven utilities is consistent regardless of the program being used (with one notable exception: the Online Help program). The <Insert> key always adds a new item or gives you a list of acceptable values to add. The <Delete> key always removes the item you have highlighted. The <Enter> key always gives you a list of items or functions associated with the object. The <F3> key allows you to rename certain items such as group names or user names. The <Escape> key always returns you back a menu or choice level.

Warning!: Never delete the group called "Everyone" as NetWare expects this group to exist and places all users in this group by default.

Jumping ahead, we can now assume that we have entered all our groups and their directory assignments, bearing in mind that as yet, we have no users defined. You now return to the menu titled **Available Topics** by pressing <Escape>.

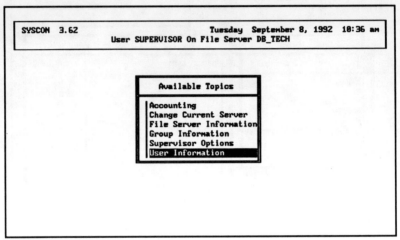

Creating User Information

To begin entering user information, highlight the option titled **User Information** and press <Enter>. You are "greeted" with a list of user names similar to the following:

By now, you are getting to be professional at this game. You know that pressing the <Insert> key on this screen starts adding new users to the system.

In our mythical installation, you add the names **Amy, Ann, Bill, Bruce, Carly, Chris, Desiree, Flip, Hank, Roy,** and **Tom**. Having performed this task, you are presented with a list of users that appear like the following:

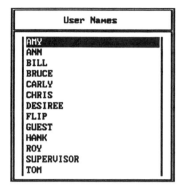

Now highlight the user named "Amy" and press <Enter>. You are then presented with a menu listing functions that you may perform with this user's object.

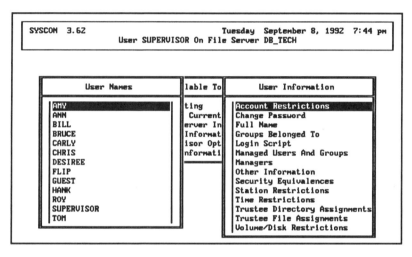

Take a little tour of some of these options and see what they do. The first option titled "Account Restrictions" determines some of the restrictions that you want to place on this user.

```
        Account Restrictions For User AMY
Account Disabled:                      No
Account Has Expiration Date:           No
   Date Account Expires:
Limit Concurrent Connections:          No
   Maximum Connections:
Allow User To Change Password:         Yes
Require Password:                      No
   Minimum Password Length:
Force Periodic Password Changes:
   Days Between Forced Changes:
   Date Password Expires:
   Limit Grace Logins:
      Grace Logins Allowed:
      Remaining Grace Logins:
Require Unique Passwords:
```

The **Account Disabled** option designates whether this person is allowed to log in to the network at all. To change this from No to Yes, type the letter **Y** and press <Enter>. If you want a user to only be able to access the network up until a specific date but no longer, you enable the option titled **Account Has Expiration Date**. If you enter a **Y** in this box, you need to fill out the option titled **Date Account Expires** with a valid date. If you do not want the user to be logged in to the network at multiple workstations at the same time, you enable the option titled **Limit Concurrent Connections**. If you have set this option to **Yes**, you have the opportunity to enter the **Maximum Connections** option. This number must be between 1 and 250 inclusive. If you want the users to alter their own passwords, you enable the option titled **Allow User To Change Password**. If you have a network where you want all users to have a password, you enable the option titled **Require Password**. If you activate that option, you will have the ability to set the **Minimum Password Length**. This determines how many letters the password must contain.

If you want your users to change their passwords on a periodic basis, you enable the option titled **Force Periodic Password Changes**. If you enable this option, you have the opportunity to alter the **Days Between Forced Changes** and **Date Password Expires**. If you want to set a limit on the number of logins the user can execute before they absolutely must change their password, you enter a **Y** in the box titled **Limit Grace Logins** and a number between 1 and 200 in the box titled **Grace Logins Allowed**. The option titled **Remaining Grace Logins** shows how many of the **Grace Logins Allowed** are unused. Enabling the option titled **Require Unique Passwords** requires that the users provide a totally new password each time they change their password. A user can change the password several times on the same day without the file server counting the passwords as previous passwords.

If you want to enter the user's password, you choose the option titled **Change Password**. You are asked to enter the password twice to verify that you entered it correctly. Only the spelling of the password is significant as NetWare passwords are recognized in both upper and lowercase (case insensitive).

The next option available is titled **Full Name**. In this box, you can type the full name of the user, i.e.: "John Quincy Public" for the user ID JOHN.

The next option titled **Groups Belonged To** is where you assign a user to a group or groups. Contrary to the title, this option shows the group(s) that the user currently belongs to, not in the past tense. Pressing <Enter> on this item shows a screen similar to the following:

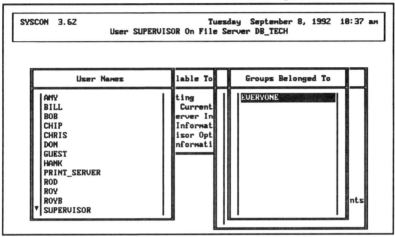

As mentioned earlier, NetWare automatically assigns each user to the group EVERYONE. If there are other groups that this user should belong to, as in our demonstration system, you would press <Insert> and be shown a list of the groups that this user doesn't belong to:

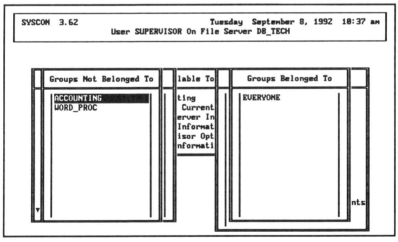

In the case of the user we are currently working on, Amy, we know that she belongs in the WORD_PROC group. To add her to that group, highlight the **WORD_PROC** entry and press <Enter>. You are then left with a **Groups Belonged To** list that appears as follows:

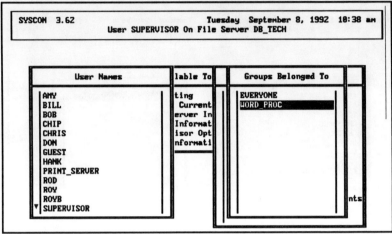

Now press <Escape> to return to your **User Information** list of functions. The next function you need to work with is **Login Script**. Before you start groaning again, please remember that we have already created our login script on paper long before we arrived here. Therefore, it is a simple matter to merely enter it into the appropriate area. To do this, press <Enter> on the **Login Script** option. If the user has no login script, a dialog appears as follows:

Login Script Does Not Exist
Read Login Script From User: AMY

Once again, there are two possible roads to travel. The path taken depends on how far along your network is configured. If you are working on a new network, there will not be any login scripts you can swipe. If this is the case, you can only press <Enter> to start a new one. If, however, your network has been running awhile and you want this user to have a similar login script to another user, all you need to do is press <Insert> and you see a screen like:

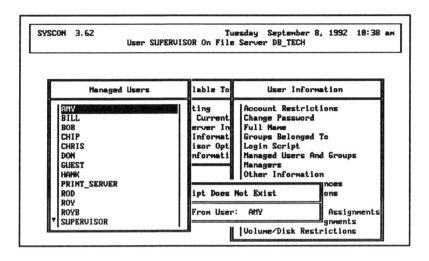

At this point, you merely select the user whose login script you think would make a good start and press <Enter> twice.

In our little house of fun, we don't have the luxury of existing login scripts to choose from, so we'll have to start from scratch. The screen in which login scripts are entered looks like this:

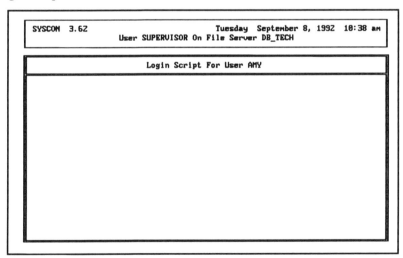

The login script screen is much like the blank screen you might see on a word processor. You can use your arrow keys to move backwards, forwards, up and down the screen. When you type, the text is inserted where your cursor is. Using the sheets created earlier, enter your login script for Amy.

When you have completed the entry of your login script, press <Escape> and you are prompted as to whether or not to save your work. If you want to save and exit, select **Yes** and press <Enter>. If you want to discard all your work, select **No** and press <Enter>. If you're not sure, press <Escape> and you return to your login script.

The option titled **Managed Users And Groups** is a method whereby you can grant a group of users the capability to manage some of the security restrictions for that group. The option titled **Managers** is used to designate which users may have access to the security access and alter who is a member of this group. For simplicity's sake, we do not cover **Managed Users And Groups** or **Managers** in this text.

The next option is titled **Security Equivalences** and this is where you can give one user the exact security rights as another user. For example, our LAN administrator on this network is named Roy and to do his job, he needs to have all the rights of the Supervisor user ID. To accomplish this, give him the security equivalence of Supervisor. When you select this option, a screen similar to the following appears:

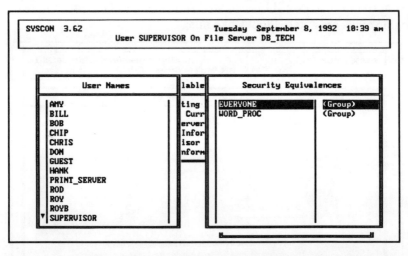

If you wish to add to this list, all you do is press <Insert> and you see a list of users and groups that this user is not equivalent to. In our example, highlight the SUPERVISOR (User) entry and press <Enter>. This leaves you with a list that appears like:

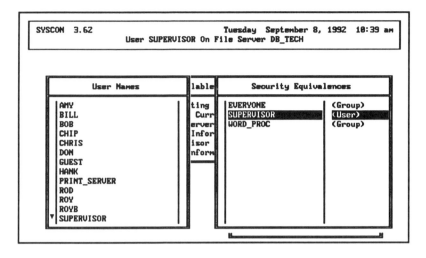

The next option on the **User Information** list of functions is titled
Station Restrictions and is used to restrict the user so that his or her
login ID may only be used in a machine with a specific *Node Address*.
This can be a rather complex thing to set up for the novice, and we do
not cover it in this text.

The option titled **Time Restrictions** is used to restrict a user's access to
the network to certain hours of the day and certain days of the week. This
information is displayed in a matrix that appears like:

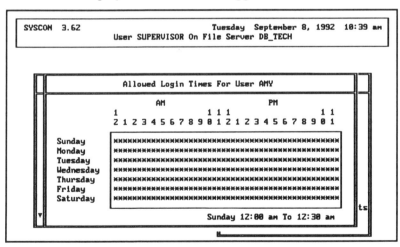

The default for user named Amy is to allow her access to the network 24
hours a day (48 half hours actually) and seven days a week. If you wanted

87

to restrict her to only being able to use the network from Monday through Saturday from the hours of 7AM until 8PM, you would use the arrow keys and spacebar to remove the asterisks (*) from the areas that she should **not** be allowed to access the network. An alternative method is to press <F5> (mark) and use the arrow keys to highlight a block of time. You then press <Delete> to remove the asterisks. To add an asterisk to a time block, you can either press <Insert> on a specific time or use <F5> to mark a block of time and then press <Insert>. *Please bear in mind that when the user's time expires, she will be kicked off the network and any attempts to log in during an unauthorized time period will be rejected.* With your settings for Amy entered, your screen appears something like:

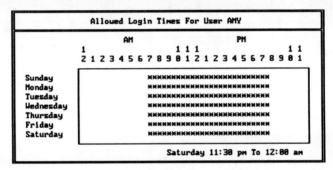

The next option is titled **Trustee Directory Assignments** and is treated in a similar fashion as the group trustee directory assignments. The main difference is that these directory assignments are for this user only. In our example, Amy needs access to a few directories to store her private files. Using the same methodology as you did for the group directory assignments, add entries for the SYS:USERS\AMY\DOCS and the SYS:USERS\AMY\WKS directories. To allow her almost total access to these directories, grant her the following rights: Read, Write, Create, Erase, and Modify. Your completed entries appear as follows:

User Names	Trustee Directory Assignments	
AMY	SYS:MAIL/10000014	[RWCEMF]
BILL	SYS:USERS\AMY\DOCS	[RWCEMF]
BOB	SYS:USERS\AMY\WKS	[RWCEMF]
CHIP		
CHRIS		
DON		
GUEST		
HANK		
PRINT_SERVER		
ROD		
ROY		
ROYB		
SUPERVISOR		

The end result of these settings is that the user has individual rights to those directories that are not part of the group's rights. If indeed there are no other users or groups with access to these directories, then the only user ID that can access these directories at any level will be Amy, the Supervisor, or someone with Supervisor Equivalence.

The next option titled **Trustee File Assignments** takes the directory assignments a step further by designating access on a file-by-file level. This can be rather complicated to manage on a user-by-user basis but it's there if you need it.

The final option is titled **Volume/Disk Restrictions** and it is used to limit the amount of hard drive space (in megabytes) that users may allocate with their files. This option can be a real lifesaver on LANs where there are many users and hard drive space is at a premium.

IN CLOSING

While this section seems to have gone on forever, we have only touched on the simplest aspects of creating and maintaining users and groups. As I stated earlier in this book, you can construct a very complex network using the functions available in NetWare 386.

SUMMARY

1. Using a paper network, start laying out the applications that will need to be accessed by the users of your network.

2. Construct groups of users based on their application and data needs. At this level, you should also know who your users are.

3. Construct login scripts appropriate to the needs of the users on paper with the NetWare installation documentation handy.

4. After logging on to the network as Supervisor, implement your groups and users using the SYSCON utility.

5. Test your configurations for each group by logging on to the network in the same manner as they would, and verify that there are no holes in security and they can access all the directories that they need to.

Section 7

NETWORK PRINTERS

WHAT ARE NETWORK PRINTERS
AND WHAT CAN YOU DO WITH THEM?

Network printers as recognized by NetWare can be any printer attached to either the file server or any of the PCs that are also attached to the network. In the good old days, older versions of NetWare restricted shared printing to only those printers that were directly attached to the file server. In this enlightened age, a network printer can be attached to a PC that a person is using for word processing, databases, and/or spreadsheets. You may also have a PC attached to the network that does nothing but service the printing needs of your network. Before we get too involved with what happens where and to whom, let's get some more handy terms out of the way.

Print Server - A PC (either the file server or a dedicated PC) that handles the printing of reports and/or documents that did not originate from that PC.

Remote Printer - A printer that is attached to a PC normally used for more functions than strictly as a print server.

Capture - A method and command line utility that takes the data that would normally flow inside your PC from memory into the printer port and redirects it to print on a printer that has been defined as a network resource.

Print Job - User initiated report(s) and/or document(s) that a user has requested to be printed on a network printer.

Print Queue - A file (or files) that keeps track of what print jobs have yet to be printed. A print queue is serviced by the PC or PCs responsible for the output assigned. The actual print queue is maintained by the file server and deletes or adds jobs as requested by network resources.

In addition to the above terms, we use some DOS and server based NetWare utilities, as follows:

PCONSOLE.EXE - A DOS based utility that is used for the creation and management of network printers and print queues.

PSERVER.NLM - A server based NLM that handles the management of the printers assigned to a network.

CAPTURE.EXE - A command line utility that allows a user to redirect LPT1, LPT2, and/or LPT3 to a network printer.

ENDCAP.EXE - A utility that disables network printer redirection.

RPRINTER.EXE - A "dual mode" utility that has both a menu and command line interface to activate the remote printing capability.

Two TSR programs are required to access a Novell network. These TSRs also allow you to redirect your output from what would normally go to a printer attached to your PC to a printer somewhere else on the network. The upside to this arrangement is that your computer returns to your control much faster since your PC is actually printing to a file instead of waiting for your printer to process the data.

One of the many benefits of network printing is that you can purchase fewer faster/better/stronger printers and still allow everyone access to them. This aspect will put a smile on any bean counter's face.

There are some decisions to be made if you are starting a new network. For example, how do you want to connect your printers to the network. If your file server is in a central location, you may want to consider attaching your network printers directly to the file server. If that scenario is not convenient for your situation, you still have some alternatives. If you have an extra PC laying around, you can make that PC into a *Dedicated Print Server*. This machine would do nothing except run a NetWare program to allow it to service the NetWare *Print Queues*. The obvious downside to this setup is that the PC cannot be used for anything else and it requires all the network hardware that any other workstation on the network does. The third alternative is to have a *Remote Printer*. This involves loading another TSR at the workstation. Ideally, this would be a PC that does not see heavy use but still needs to be available as a workstation. This workstation should also be in a convenient location that is accessible.

You can also use any combination of the three for that custom approach. The course you choose should be driven by several factors. Office layout is one of the prime factors involved. If your file server is in a fairly wide open area, the file server approach may be the best. In an office where there are extra PCs laying around unused and the file server method would not be convenient, the dedicated print server could be a valid option. In an office where there are no extra PCs and the file server method won't work, the remote printer method could do the trick.

In this section, we touch on all three methods to give you some background for making the right choices.

THE BASICS

Network printers are very simple in concept to configure and implement. Assuming you have the specific printers picked out, all you have to do is create print queues to service them and a method to service the print queues. That didn't hurt, did it? The real world is not too much worse than the concept. The biggest problem you will encounter with setting up network printers involves the hardware, not the software.

GET THE HARDWARE RIGHT

The most common method of attaching any kind of printer to any kind of PC is through the parallel port. The main problem you encounter with this setup is the parallel port settings not matching the specifications. This could involve both the I/O port and the interrupt being set incorrectly. DOS has a nasty habit of fixing the first parallel port to be LPT1 almost without regard to its real setting. For example, if you have a parallel port physically configured as LPT2 and there is no LPT1 in the system, DOS will make it behave as if it were set up as LPT1. Therefore, it is very important that whatever system your network printers are attached to has had the printer ports checked, verified, and tested.

In our sample network, we have two printers that we attach to the network: a high speed dot matrix printer for database reports and spreadsheets, and a laser printer for word processing and presentation type reports.

As you did when you created the users and groups, make sure you are attached to the network and logged in as SUPERVISOR. Having completed this strenuous task, you are now ready to get to work.

DOING THE DEED

The main program used to configure your network printers is called PCONSOLE.EXE. This is a DOS based menu driven Novell utility that behaves the same as the other NetWare programs we have used. To invoke the PCONSOLE utility type **PCONSOLE** and press <Enter> at the DOS prompt. You are greeted with a screen that appears as follows:

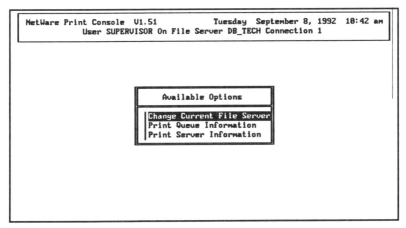

There are three options at the main level. The option titled **Change Current File Server** applies if you are working in a multiple server environment. Use **Print Queue Information** to define and manage the print queues. The last option titled **Print Server Information** is where you define and manage the print server(s) that you need.

PRINT QUEUES AND SERVERS

The first step in setting up network printers is to select the option titled **Print Queue Information** and press <Enter>. The lack of any names in the Print Queue box indicates that you need to add some. To accomplish this, press <Insert> and give the print queue a name. In our fictitious network, you need two print queues to service our two network printers. The print queues we create are called DOT_MATRIX and LASER. A good rule of thumb regarding the naming of print queues is to make the names descriptive. After adding the two queues, you now have a list of print queues that appears as follows:

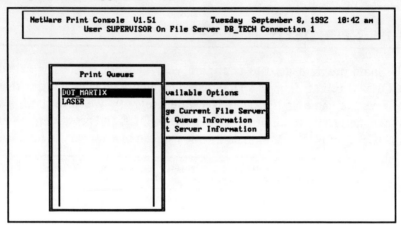

Now that you have defined your print queues, you are finished with them for the moment. You define a single print server to handle both printers on our fictional network. To do this, press <Escape> to return to the main menu and select the option titled **Print Server Information** and press <Enter>.

You only need to create a single print server to handle your two printers since NetWare is smart enough to handle the situation without designating a separate print server for each printer. Pressing <Insert>, fill in the name of your print server into the box. Your print server is called PSERV. After entering the print server name, the screen now appears as follows:

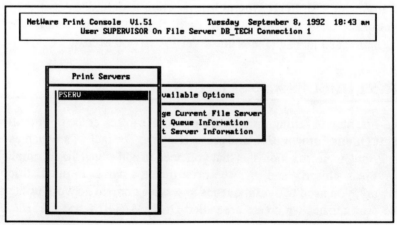

To begin configuring the print server, press <Enter> with the highlight on the print server name. This presents the following screen.

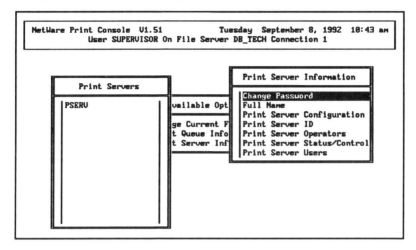

The first option titled **Change Password** allows you to assign a password to that print server. If you give your print server a password, you will have to supply this password whenever you start your print server. This can be a hassle at times so you avoid it for now. The next option titled **Full Name** is a means by which you can give your print server a descriptive and more verbose name.

The next option titled **Print Server Configuration** is where you access the meat of the configuration. Pressing <Enter> on this item produces the following screen.

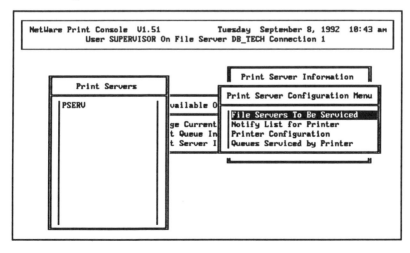

The Print Server Configuration Menu is where you set up the physical aspects of the print server. The first option titled **File Servers To Be Serviced** is where you designate which file servers are going to be able to access this print server. Pressing <Enter> on this option produces a screen similar to the following:

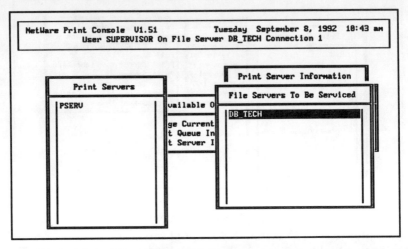

If your file server does not appear in this list, press <Insert> and select it from a list of candidates that appears. To exit this list, pressing <Escape> returns you to the Print Server Configuration Menu.

The next option is titled **Printer Configuration** and is used to set the actual printer ports that your printers are attached to. Pressing <Enter> on this option produces a screen similar to the following:

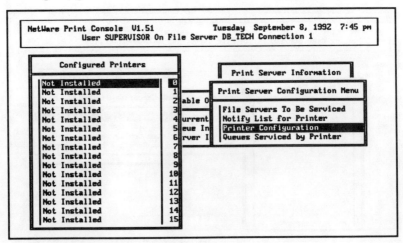

The **Configured Printers** list shows the printer numbers and the names associated with them. To simplify matters, NetWare allows you to reference the printers attached to a print server by their numbers.

Pressing <Enter> on the entry for the item titled **Not Installed 0** allows you to start setting up the characteristics for this printer. The following dialog appears:

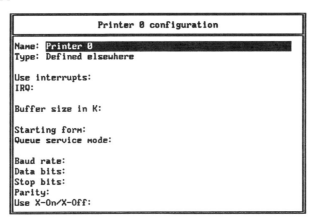

The first item to fill out on this screen is the printer name. NetWare defaults this to read Printer 0 and I suggest that you leave it this way. The next option titled **Type** refers the I/O port of the printer and the location of that printer port. Pressing <Enter> on this field brings up a screen similar to the following:

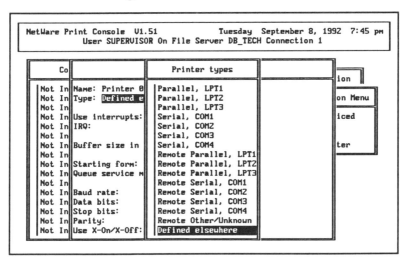

97

As you can see, there are many types to choose from. When NetWare shows printer type as **Remote**, this is meant to indicate that the printer port does not reside inside the file server itself.

Since this is the dot matrix printer, which is going to be attached to the file server, make sure that the highlight is on the item labeled **Parallel, LPT1**. When you press <Enter> on the port, you arrive at the prompt marked **Use interrupts:**. Leave this at "Yes" since you want the print server to have an absolute method of finding your printer port. At this point, the screen should appear as follows:

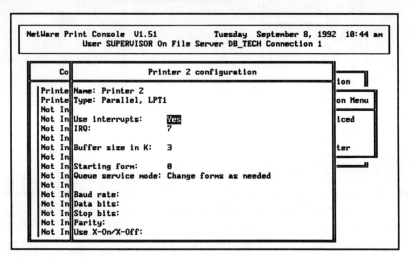

Since you are going to run the rest of the options at their default, press <Escape> and choose the option label "Yes" when asked to save the settings.

To set up the laser printer to be used on a remote workstation as a shared printer, arrow key down to the next available printer on your list, and press <Enter> on the next available printer number that shows as **Not Installed**. You are now presented with the same set of screens as outlined previously. Instead of selecting the option labeled **Parallel, LPT1**, select the option titled **Remote Parallel, LPT1**. This leaves a screen as follows:

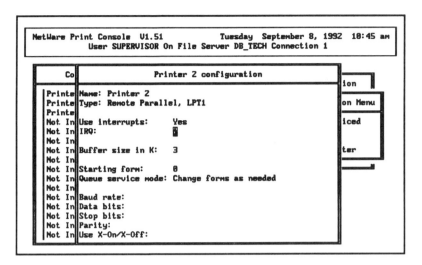

Pressing <Escape> and again answering "Yes" to the prompt saves all of your settings.

Now press <Escape> to return to the Print Server Configuration Menu and choose the option labeled **Queues Serviced by Printer**. This brings up a screen that appears as follows:

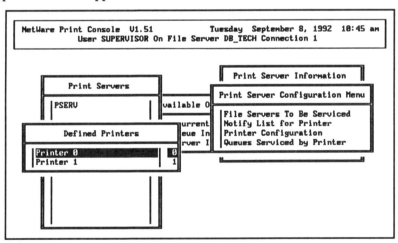

Select **Printer 0** and press <Enter>. Press <Insert> and you are presented with a list of eligible Queues that you may attach to this printer.

From the Available Queues list, select the queue named **DOT_MATRIX** and press <Enter>. You are then asked for the priority to assign to this queue for this port.

Since there will be only one queue for this port, leave the setting at "1" (the highest priority) and press <Enter>. This leaves a screen that appears as follows:

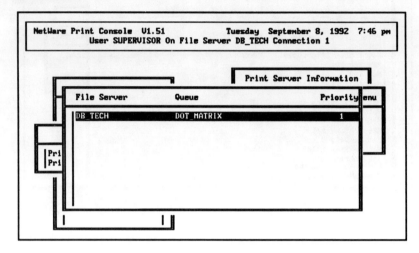

Now press <Escape> six times and press <Enter> once to exit out of this program. We can now test our configuration.

OBSERVE WHAT WE HATH WROUGHT

Since you have configured your *Print Server*, the next step is to test the work you have performed in the PCONSOLE utility.

You first need to make sure that both printers are properly attached to the relevant machines. In our test network, this means that the dot matrix printer is attached to the file server's LPT1 port and that the laser printer is attached to a workstation.

On the file server, make sure that you are at the colon (:) prompt. If this is not the case, press <Alt><Escape> until you are at the proper prompt. Next type the following and press <Enter>:

LOAD PSERVER PSERV

If all has gone well, you should see a screen like the following:

```
                    Novell NetWare Print Server V1.22
                          Server PSERV Running

  0: Printer 0                      4: Not installed
     Not connected


  1: Printer 1                      5: Not installed
     Not connected


  2: Not installed                 6: Not installed


  3: Not installed                 7: Not installed
```

This indicates that the NetWare Loadable Module that controls the print server has initialized properly. If you received an error message of any kind, this indicates that there was something misentered in the PCONSOLE program. If this is the case, please go back and verify that your settings are all correct.

The next thing to do is test whether or not our configuration is actually working as advertised. To accomplish this, we make use of two NetWare command line utilities. The first utility we explore is called CAPTURE.EXE. This utility controls all the print redirection that needs to occur between your local printer port to the file server. You should still be logged on to the file server at this point.

The capture capability is enabled through the use of the two NetWare TSRs that you use to attach to the network. This gives NetWare the capability of "capturing" the output that DOS would normally send to your printer port (which doesn't have to exist) to a queue that exists on the file server. The capture command can only be used on parallel ports; the redirection of serial ports is not supported in NetWare 386 version 3.11 or 4.0.

To disable network printing and end the CAPTURE redirection, NetWare provides a utility called ENDCAP.EXE. ENDCAP has no parameters and no menu interface.

As with many command line utilities, there are many options that you should be aware of. The format of the capture command is as follows:

CAPTURE <options>

While some of the options can be labeled as esoteric, we present all the options for your information. The options consist of the following:

/SHow - This option shows the current status of your LPT ports and what current options are enabled if you have printer redirection enabled. The short form of this command is /SH.

/Job=jobname - Jobname is the name of a print configuration that you may have set up using the PRINTCON utility. The PRINTCON utility is not covered in this text due to the complexity of configuration and management. The short form of this command is /J=.

/Server=fileserver - In a multiple file server environment, this option can be used to send your print job to a print queue that is managed by another file server. If this parameter is omitted, it assumes the current file server where you executed the command from. The short form of this command is /S=.

/Queue=queuename - This is where you would supply the name of the print queue that you wish to print to. If this option is omitted, your print will be redirected to the printer that is set up as "Printer 0" on the file server. The short form of this command is /Q=.

/Local=n - This option indicates which parallel port to capture. This is a number between 1 and 3 inclusive. This parameter defaults to 1 indicating that LPT1 is to be redirected. The short form of this command is /L=.

/Form=form or n - This is the name of the form you wish to print on. The forms are created and managed with the PRINTDEF utility. Due to the complexity of the PRINTDEF utility, we will not be covering it in this text. The short form of this command is /F=.

/CReate=path - This option is used to redirect your output to a file. This file must conform to DOS naming standards and the path must be on the file server. The short form of this command is /CR=.

/Copies=n (1-999) - This option can be used to control the number of copies that will be printed of your text. This option defaults to 1 copy if it is omitted. The short form of this command is /C=.

/TImeout=n - This option allows you to print from an application without exiting the application. In essence, this option is a timer that goes off when your workstation is finished printing to the queue. After the timeout period (in seconds) expires, the print job is released to the queue so that the printer may begin servicing your print request. The short form of this command is /TI=.

/Keep - This option comes in handy if you have a print job that may take several hours to complete. This option makes sure that the file server keeps all the data that it receives from your workstation in case your workstation is taken off the network by a power loss or other calamity. When the server recognizes that your workstation is no longer connected to the network, it sends the data to the printer. The short form of this command is /K.

/Tabs=n (1-18) - This option is used only when your application doesn't have a print formatter. This option will convert any tab characters it encounters in a printout to spaces. The default for this option is to convert every tab character into eight spaces. The short form of this command is /T=.

/No Tabs - This option ensures that the data you send to the printer is not changed by the NetWare queue. In essence, this tells the queue that the data coming down the line should be treated as binary data and to process it as is. A good example of this would be the printing of a chart from a spreadsheet. The short form of this command is /TI=.

/Banner=bannername - A word or phrase of up to 12 characters that may appear on the banner page of your printout. A banner page is a page that precedes your print job and contains the date and time the printout was sent. The short form of this command is /B=.

/NAMe=name - This can be a word or phrase of up to 12 characters that can be used to describe who sent the print job. By default, this is set to the name of the user who sent the print job. The short form of this command is /NAM=.

/No Banner - This option disables the banner page feature of NetWare. The short form of this command is /NB.

/FormFeed - This option tells the printer to print the next print job at the top of the next sheet of paper. This is useful for programs that do not eject the last page after printing, such as some older spreadsheet programs.

This option is the default if the /No Form Feed option is omitted. The short form of this command is /FF.

/No FormFeed - This option tells the printer to assume that the application will eject the last page after it is finished printing. Most word processors would be such a program. The short form of this command is /NFF.

/AUtoendcap - This option sends the data to the network printer when you enter or exit an application. By default, this option is enabled. The short form of this command is /AU.

/No Autoend - This option will not release the data to the printer when you enter or exit an application. The short form of this command is /NA.

/NOTIfy - This option is used to notify the user who sent the print job when that job is finished printing. The short form of this command is /NOTI.

/No NOTIfy - This option will not notify the user when the print job is completed. This option is the default setting and the short form of the command is /NNOTI.

/DOmain=domain - This option is used in a server environment where domains have been declared. This is normally used only on very large and complex network systems. The short form of this command is /DO=.

While this may seem quite a daunting list of parameters to remember, very rarely are all of them used on a single command line. In order to simplify your (possible) quandary over the use of CAPTURE, here are some sample uses of the CAPTURE command.

For a spreadsheet program where no graphics are to be printed:

CAPTURE /Q=DOT_MATRIX /FF /TI=5

The command above redirects output to the DOT_MATRIX queue with form feeds added to the end of every print job and a time interval of five seconds between the end of the print request and the releasing of the print job to the queue.

For the same spreadsheet program where there would be graphics printed, the command might read:

CAPTURE /Q=DOT_MATRIX /FF /NT

The major difference between the two commands is the deletion of the /TI parameter to give the spooler long enough to process the data and the addition of the /NT command to tell the spooler that binary data is coming down the line.

For a word processing program that doesn't support NetWare (I've heard that there are still one or two of them left), the command might read as follows:

CAPTURE /Q=LASER /NFF /NT /TI=5

The above command redirects the printer output to the queue called LASER, suppresses the form feed at the end of the print job, specifies no conversion of tab characters (binary stream), and sets the timeout interval at five seconds.

As you can see, there are many possible permutations to the capture command with only a few that you will probably use from day to day. Once again, strict adherence to the K.I.S.S. principle will pay off in the long run with fewer migraine headaches.

To test our print configuration, we perform some simple commands to test the network printer operations. At this point, we assume the following:

1. The file server is running the NetWare operating system and the PSERVER NLM is loaded properly.

2. The printer is attached to the file server, that it has a good connection, and that it is online and waiting for a print job.

3. You are logged in to the file server as supervisor and have a path to the SYS:PUBLIC directory.

The easiest testing method is the old trusty Print Screen method. To perform this function, do the following steps from whatever network directory you are currently in:

1. Type the following: **CAPTURE /Q=DOT_MATRIX /FF** and press <Enter>. You should see a response similar to the following:

```
F:\PUBLIC>CAPTURE /Q=DOT_MATRIX /FF
Device LPT1: re-routed to queue DOT_MATRIX on server RN_ADAY.
```

2. Type **DIR /W** and press <Enter>.

3. When you are returned to the DOS prompt, press <Shift><Print Scrn>. You should see the cursor travel the entire screen and then return to the DOS prompt.

4. At the DOS prompt, type **ENDCAP** and press <Enter>.

Your network printer should now start printing the screen that you observed at the end of step 3.

Tie the Knot

The use of the CAPTURE and the ENDCAP programs is normally hidden from the end user through the use of batch files, menu scripts, etc.

Let's take the example given above for the spreadsheet program. A sample batch file called 321.BAT might look like the following:

```
@ECHO OFF
Rem ----- Batch File To Start the 321 SpreadSheet
G:
CAPTURE /Q=DOT_MATRIX /FF /TI=5
321
ENDCAP
F:
```

Please bear in mind that this is a rather simple use of the capture command and your needs will vary from program to program and user to user.

BUY 10 LASERS FOR THE PRICE OF ONE

The next issue we tackle is that of the remote printer. By definition, this is a printer that is remote from the file server. Go figure. The perfect remote printer PC candidate is one that does not see very heavy use and is unlikely to be rebooted very often. A prime example of this type of use would be that of a receptionist or other person who normally is in one application all day, and there is very little chance of something going wrong.

If we can call the engine of the remote printing capability the PSERVER NLM, then certainly the wheels of the bus would be the RPRINTER.EXE utility. The PSERVER utility is rather unique in that it can be either a command line driven or a menu driven utility. We will be exploring both uses of RPRINTER; however, we first examine the use of the menu driven method.

RCONSOLE - The Menu Path

From the workstation to which the laser printer is attached, make sure that the workstation is logged with the User ID that will normally be used for that workstation. The execution of the menu driven aspects of the RPRINTER utility are very simple. At the DOS prompt type **RPRINTER** and press <Enter>.

You should see a screen similar to the following that lists all of the available print servers:

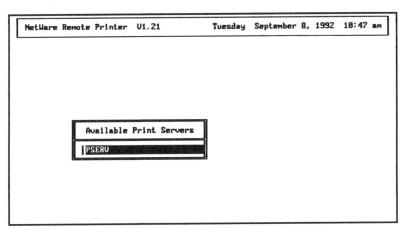

Since you only have one print server defined for this network, press <Enter> on the one labeled PSERV. Accomplishing this action brings you to the next screen which consists of a list of available printers for the print server. This screen could appear as follows:

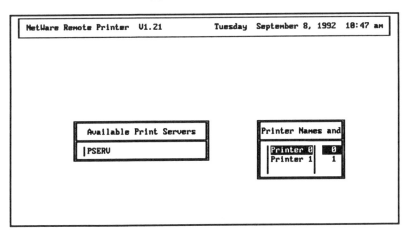

Since you have already allocated one of the printers to the file server (printer 0), there is only one printer to choose from. Pressing <Enter> on this printer activates the RPRINTER program and presents you with a message similar to the following:

*** Remote Printer "Printer 1" (printer 1) installed ***

You can now test the operation of your remote printer in the same manner used to test the printer connected to the file server. Remember, however, that the name of the queue would be different since this printer is to service a different queue. For example, the capture command might read:

CAPTURE /Q=LASER /FF

Deactivating the remote printer attached to this workstation can only be accomplished via the command line interface to RPRINTER.

Note: While the workstation is running the RPRINTER program, all print jobs that originate from that PC should be routed through the NetWare print queues using the CAPTURE command or similar utility.

The other method used to activate RPRINTER is the command line method. This method works very well for a user's login script and can also be used to deactivate the remote printer capability. The parameters that RPRINTER is looking for are as follows:

RPRINTER PSERV 1

The command above tells RPRINTER that the print server you wish to use is called PSERV and it is going to support printer number 1.

To deactivate remote printing for this workstation and remove RPRINTER from memory type the following:

RPRINTER PSERV 1 -r

The command above tells RPRINTER that the print server you wish to use is called PSERV, you are going to do something with printer 1, and that something is to remove it (-r).

Yeah, But How Do I Remember All This Junk?

Knowing how to do all this neat stuff at the DOS prompt is all well and good; however, to make your life easier, you really should write some of this stuff down. The absolute best place to do this is in the one place where it can do the most good. For example, to get the file server to load the PSERVER NLM every time it starts up, you would add a line to your server AUTOEXEC.NCF file. To do this, you should be logged in to the network as SUPERVISOR and use the SYSCON utility. The option you should look for is the one labeled **Supervisor Options** and then the one labeled **Edit System AUTOEXEC File**. Place the following (or similar) line in your AUTOEXEC.NCF as follows:

LOAD PSERVER PSERV

For the User ID logging on with the PC that will act as the remote printer, add the following (or similar) line to their login script (after performing the search drive mappings).

#RPRINTER PSERV 1

By performing the two steps above to save your work, you have automated all that distasteful DOS command line junk that we love so well.

SUMMARY

1. Using PCONSOLE, define the print queues that you will need to service. Remember to name them descriptively to avoid confusion.

2. While still in PCONSOLE, give your print server a name.

3. Configure your print server to use the relevant local and remote (to the file server) printer ports.

4. Load the NLM on the file server to activate your network printing.

5. Making sure that all your printers are properly attached, begin testing their functionality by using NetWare's CAPTURE, ENDCAP, and RPRINTER commands.

6. Using SYSCON, save the proper commands to start the network printing in the system AUTOEXEC.NCF file and the remote workstation login script(s).

Section 8

SETTING UP YOUR APPLICATIONS

Now that we have muddled through the majority of the mundane part of
the installation and/or configuration of NetWare, it's time to get down to
business. The business at hand is installing and configuring some
applications for use on your network.

THE INSIDE STORY

The vast majority of networks out there in the real world are used for
extremely boring (but very important) things. There are countless
networks across the globe whose sole purpose is to provide a convenient
method to run word processing. Chances are, most networks that you run
across are used as a giant floppy disk to store data in a place where anyone
can get to it. That is not to say that these giant floppy disks aren't
absolutely vital to the business world.

Conversely, there are many LANs that have enough different types of
software installed to truly boggle the mind. As an example, many
attorneys have automated their offices to an amazing degree. On a typical
attorney network, you might find the following types of software:

Word Processing - In an industry whose sole purpose seems at times to
generate documents, this is a given.

Time and Billing - The next major thing attorneys generate is bills and
they expect them to be paid. Go figure.

Accounting - Attorneys have some very demanding needs in the
accounting area. If it is not done correctly, they could lose their license
or go to jail, so they pay a lot of attention (and money) to this need.

Custom Hardware Interfaces - Many offices have an interface to their phone system, copy machines, etc. to facilitate the billing process and recover every possible cost.

Spreadsheets - While nowhere near as popular as word processing, there are some needs for spreadsheet analysis for income forecasting and other number crunching.

Databases - Over the course of time, attorneys gather a vast amount of information, and they want some sort of access to this information.

Miscellaneous - This is probably the broadest category of software known to man. Some attorneys collect "nick knack" software the way some people collect memorabilia. It doesn't matter whether it works or not, what really matters is that it is cheap.

Ok, so you're sitting there saying, "Hey, good for them, but who really cares?" Well, some poor fool had to install and configure all this stuff. Sometimes that unfortunate person works for the company that sold them the hardware. Many times, it falls on the local PC guru to perform this task. *Note: The local PC guru might consist of the one person in the office who is capable of turning on his or her machine without referring to the instruction manual.* While some of these packages are a breeze to install, others have all the ambiance of changing the baby's diaper. It's a smelly job but no one else is going to do it, and it may grow into something useful.

DO THE RIGHT THING

In the past few years, there have been tremendous strides made in installation programs. Many of these also take into account that there may be a network handy; some of them even have readable documentation. In installing or configuring software, the very first step you should ever take is to read the manual.

If this is a new network installation or merely the installation (or upgrade) of a package, you should spend plenty of time planning your work. You should also know what users (or groups) are going to need access to this software and just how much access they really need. You may need to grant additional access rights to your file server and have many login scripts to alter.

GENERAL RULES TO LIVE BY

1. **Read the Manual.**

2. Make backup copies of the installation diskettes using the DOS DISKCOPY command if possible. This may seem foolish since you might have shiny new diskettes in your hands; however, remember that Murphy's laws were written with computers in mind.
   Note: Please refer to your license agreement and your installation instructions to determine whether this is allowed. If you have a standard license agreement, then you did not buy the software; you merely paid for the honor of using it on a specific number of PCs.

3. Always install software while logged in to the network as SUPERVISOR. Almost all software installation involves the creation of directories and subdirectories, and you will need the proper access to be able to accomplish this.

4. Take your time and take notes. Sometimes things can happen that you might not remember later. There are many packages out there that require 10 to 15 diskettes for installation, and you want to be able to back track if you encounter some problems. This can also be helpful if you need help with the installation.

5. When in doubt, exit out. If something doesn't seem right and you are receiving some error messages, get the heck out of Dodge and regroup.

6. Make sure your software license covers the actual number of people who are going to use the software. The software police take a dim view of people who bypass the software licensing requirements (yes, there are software police).

THE BASICS

There are two things that almost all software requires. A place to store the programs and a place to store the data. In keeping with this theme, there are three basic methods for configuring your software. The first method is what I call the *Bucket Method*. This means that all programs and data reside in the same directory. This method should only be considered for applications that have a very strict method for dealing with data. By that, I mean that the user is really unaware of what the program is doing with the data and has no capability to alter any other files in the directory other than what the application decides to alter.

The second method could be called the *Universal Method*. By this, I mean that there is a *search path* or search drive mapped to the directory that contains the programs, and the program doesn't care which directory you execute the application from. This method is typically used for word processing and database applications.

The third method might be called the *Fool It Method*. This is typically used for spreadsheet type programs. The driving philosophy behind this method is that you tell the program the drive letter where the data is stored but not the directory. For example, in a spreadsheet program, you may tell the program's configuration that it should look for spreadsheets on drive G:. Due to the flexibility of NetWare's drive mapping, drive G: could be set to a different directory for each user. Some software may have specific drivers required for a particular workstation's monitor or printer setup, so you can sometimes keep the configuration file(s) in a search directory as well.

Once again, the documentation that came with your software should give you a hint as to which method should be employed. Due to the millions of different software packages out there, the installation instructions can be your friend in a time of trouble.

SAFE COMPUTING

Once you have installed and tested your software, it is a good idea to make the executables (normally files with an extension of EXE or COM) read only to prohibit "accidental" deletion. The preferred method of doing this is with NetWare's FLAG.EXE program.

To flag programs as shareable and read only (no deleting) you should perform the following:

1. Change directories to where the executables are kept. You should also be logged in as SUPERVISOR.

2. At the DOS prompt, type the following and press <Enter> after each line.

   FLAG *.EXE SRO

   FLAG *.COM SRO

This makes sure that the executables are set as **Sharable Read Only.**

The notable exception to this is the case where you have self-modifying executables. Your manual will normally tell you if this is the case and what files are affected. If you do run across this problem, merely perform the following where <FileName.Ext> is the name of the file to be modified:

> **FLAG <FileName.Ext> SRW**

This command sets the file as Shareable **Read Write.**

NOW WHAT

At this stage, you will want to make sure that the application works properly for the users who intend to use it. This should be done one at a time at first so that you may retain some sort of control over the process. After you have successfully tested the users one at a time, start letting them in two or three at a time. If, at this point, there are still no problems, take a break to relax and then let them attack it at will.

Appendix A

SAMPLE ELECTRONIC MAIL PROGRAM

Included with this book is a sample network utility and electronic mail program. This program is provided as is with no guarantee as to suitability and/or functionality. This program may only be used by the purchaser of this book and distribution of this software is limited to the same.

INSTALLATION

To install the sample program, you should be logged in to the file server as SUPERVISOR and be residing at the root directory of volume SYS. At the DOS prompt, insert the installation diskette into a floppy drive and type either **A:INSTALL** or **B:INSTALL** (depending upon where the diskette is located) and press <Enter>. You should type the network drive letter where you want to install the program, and you should probably leave the directory as is. The installation program prompts you to continue the installation process. Upon completion of the installation process, the installation program creates the necessary data files for you and gathers a list of all the users defined in your network and inserts them into your E-Mail user database.

CONFIGURATION

There are some things you need to configure to utilize the program to its maximum potential. You should have a list of applications you want to execute by this point. The first step in configuration is to execute the program named DBCONFIG in the directory created by the installation program. You are greeted by a screen similar to the following:

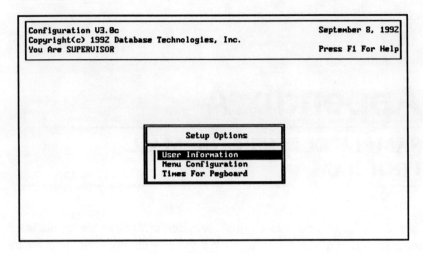

```
Configuration U3.8c                              September 8, 1992
Copyright(c) 1992 Database Technologies, Inc.
You Are SUPERVISOR                               Press F1 For Help




                         ┌─────────────────────────┐
                         │      Setup Options       │
                         ├─────────────────────────┤
                         │ User Information         │
                         │ Menu Configuration       │
                         │ Times For Pegboard       │
                         └─────────────────────────┘
```

The option titled **User Information** is used to add new users to the menu and E-Mail system. All users defined are added to the system upon installation, however subsequent users that are created in NetWare are not automatically added in. The second option, titled **Menu Configuration**, is used to alter and manage the menu entries that your users may need. The final option is called **Times For Pegboard** and is used to set up return times for people.

Setting Up Users

Selecting the option titled **User Information** presents you with a list of users that are authorized to use the E-Mail and menu functions. To add a new user, you press <Insert>. To change a user's information, highlight that user and press <Enter>. To delete a user, highlight the user to delete and press <Delete>. When you add or change a user, you are presented with a screen similar to the following:

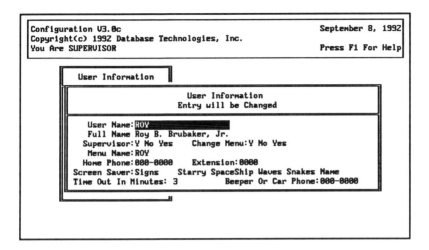

```
Configuration U3.8c                              September 8, 1992
Copyright(c) 1992 Database Technologies, Inc.
You Are SUPERVISOR                               Press F1 For Help
```

```
  User Information

              User Information
              Entry will be Changed

  User Name: ROY
  Full Name Roy B. Brubaker, Jr.
  Supervisor: Y No Yes     Change Menu: Y No Yes
  Menu Name: ROY
  Home Phone: 000-0000     Extension: 0000
  Screen Saver: Signs     Starry SpaceShip Waves Snakes Name
  Time Out In Minutes: 3            Beeper Or Car Phone: 000-0000
```

The first data entry area is for the network user ID. The next entry space is for the full name of the user. The option titled **Supervisor** has two possible answers, and you may change the answer by using the left and right arrow key. The **Supervisor** option is used to designate those users who may execute the DBCONFIG program and alter user information. Understandably, this option should be restricted to a select few. The option titled **Change Menu** is used to determine whether or not this user may add, change, or delete menu entries. The option titled **Menu Name** is used to enter the name of the menu entries that the user may select from. If you are not sure what menus are defined, you may press <F10> on this field and select from a list of menus already defined.

The options titled **Home Phone, Extension,** and **Beeper Or Car Phone** are used by the employee tracking portion of the menu. The option titled **Screen Saver** will allow you to choose from one of five screen savers that may be activated in the menu program. The program defaults to a nighttime-like scene with occasional thunderbolts. The option titled **Time Out In Minutes** is used to set the number of minutes after no keyboard activity that the screen saver will activate. To deactivate the screen savers, enter a 0 (zero) in the field.

Menu Options

Each user is assigned a set of menu options that share a specific name. When the installation program creates the users, it assigns them a menu named SHARED. You are of course free to change this in the user information. To add new menu options, select the option titled **Menu**

Configuration from the main menu. This presents a list of defined users and the names of their menus. Highlight the user that has the menu you want to alter and press <Enter> to get a list of the menu options available. If this is a new installation, you are automatically prompted to add a new entry. This screen appears as follows:

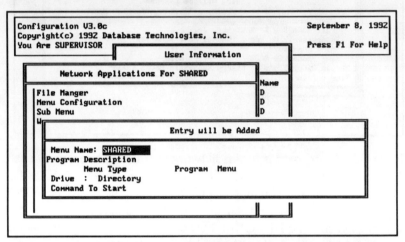

The first field is for the name of the menu to which this entry should be attached. The next field is for a brief description of the entry. The next field is used to determine whether this is a program item or a submenu heading. If you choose the option titled **Menu Type**, you are prompted to enter a submenu name. If you have chosen this to be a submenu, you should press <Enter> past the remaining fields. If you have chosen this to be a **Program Menu** item, you should enter the drive letter that you have mapped for this program. The next field is labeled **Directory** and should be used to indicate the directory you want to execute the program from. The final option labeled **Command To Start** is used to enter the command you would enter from the DOS prompt to execute the program.

If you have many entries that are to be common across many menus, you may press <Ctrl-G> at the list of menu entries and choose from any of the items to copy to the menu that you are currently working in.

USING THE PROGRAM

To execute the menu and E-Mail program, you should enter **DMENU** in the directory where you installed the package. Remember that <F1> activates the help system throughout the program. Entering the program presents you with a screen similar to the following:

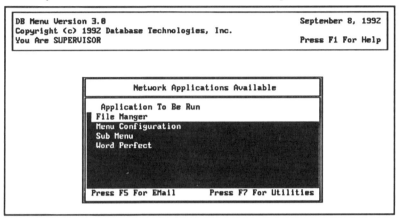

```
DB Menu Version 3.0                              September 8, 1992
Copyright (c) 1992 Database Technologies, Inc.
You Are SUPERVISOR                               Press F1 For Help



                   Network Applications Available

             Application To Be Run
             File Manger
             Menu Configuration
             Sub Menu
             Word Perfect



         Press F5 For EMail       Press F7 For Utilities
```

If you have allowed your users to alter their menus, then the following keyboard commands are applicable: <Insert> to add new entries, <Delete> to delete entries, <Enter> to execute the program highlighted, and <F10> to change the entry. If your user is not allowed to alter the menu, pressing <Insert>, <Delete>, or <F10> will produce the proverbial brick wall.

Pressing <F5> allows you to access the E-Mail functions. This is presented via the following screen:

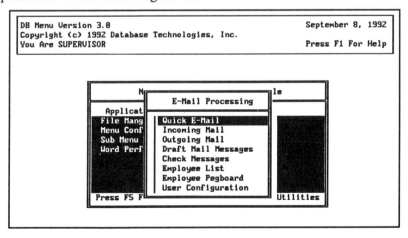

```
DB Menu Version 3.0                              September 8, 1992
Copyright (c) 1992 Database Technologies, Inc.
You Are SUPERVISOR                               Press F1 For Help



                   N┌─────────────────────────┐le
            Applicat│    E-Mail Processing    │
            File Mang│ Quick E-Mail            │
            Menu Conf│ Incoming Mail           │
            Sub Menu │ Outgoing Mail           │
            Word Perf│ Draft Mail Messages     │
                     │ Check Messages          │
                     │ Employee List           │
                     │ Employee Pegboard       │
                     │ User Configuration      │
            Press F5 F└─────────────────────────┘Utilities
```

119

The first option labeled **Quick E-Mail** is used to send a fast phone type message to a user. You are first presented with a list of users defined in the system; use the arrow keys to highlight the user to send mail to and press <Enter>. You then see a screen like:

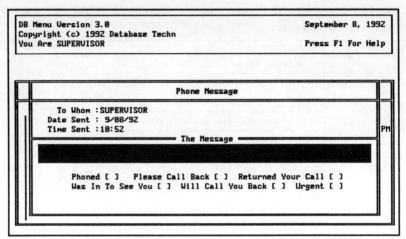

You then type the message that you want the person to receive. After entering the message, choose from any of the boxes marked with brackets ([ ]). Enter any letter in the box and it will be converted to a check mark (✔). Pressing <Enter> after the last box sends the message to the user.

The next option on the E-Mail menu is labeled **Incoming Mail**. This is where you check your incoming mail. You use <Delete> to delete old mail, <Enter> to view the message, or <F7> to print out your mail. The option titled **Outgoing Mail** is used to compose and send mail to other users. Pressing <Insert> produces the following screen:

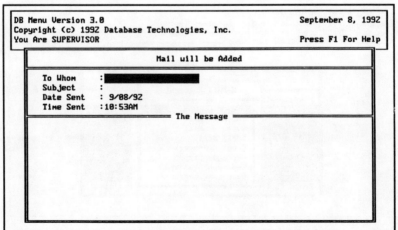

In the field marked **To Whom** you can either enter the user name or group name to send the mail to or leave it blank to call up a pop-up menu of items to choose from. Pressing <Enter> once you have entered the subject places you in the message area. This area can store up to 1050 characters of text. When you have completed the message, you must press <Ctrl-Enter> to save the message and send it.

IN CLOSING

The remainder of the menu options can be explored at your leisure. This program is intended to be used as an aid to your day-to-day work and we sincerely hope that you can find some use for it. All correspondence regarding this program should be sent to the publisher for forwarding to the author.

Appendix B

INSTALLATION WORKSHEET

File Server Worksheet

File Server Name _____ Installed by _____ On _____

Make/Model _____ Bought from _____

Memory: Base _____ Extended _____

Hard Drive Controller _____ Hardware Setting _____

Novell Driver _____

First Hard Drive

CMOS Type _____ Capacity _____

Maker _____ Model _____

Second Hard Drive

CMOS Type _____ Capacity _____

Maker _____ Model _____

Video Card Type _____

I/O Board Settings: Type_____Irq_____   Port_____

                      Type_____Irq_____   Port_____

Network Boards: Net___ Type_____ Irq___ Port___ Driver_____

                Net___ Type_____ Irq___ Port___ Driver_____

                Net___ Type_____ Irq___ Port___ Driver_____

                Net___ Type_____ Irq___ Port___ Driver_____

Floppy Drive Type: Drive A _____   Drive B _____

Server Boot Method: Diskette_____   Hard Drive _____

Novell Version _____   Number of Users _____

Workstation Configuration Worksheet

Workstation in Use By _____ Serial # _____

Type of Workstation _____ DOS Version _____

Floppy Drive Type: A _____   B _____

Hard Drive Type: 1 _____   2 _____

    CMOS Type   _____   _____

Network Interface Installed By _____ On _____

Memory _____ I/O Port _____ Interrupt _____ Address _____

Other Cards Installed _____

_____

_____

Index

Other Books from Wordware Publishing, Inc.

Popular Applications Series
Build Your Own Computer
Cost Control Using Lotus 1-2-3
Creating Newsletters with Ventura
Database Publishing with Ventura
Desktop Publishing with Word 2.0 for
   Windows
Desktop Publishing with WordPerfect
   for Windows
Learn AmiPro 3.0 in a Day
Learn AutoCAD in a Day
Learn AutoCAD 12 in a Day
Learn C in Three Days
Learn CorelDRAW! in a Day
Learn DataPerfect in a Day
Learn dBASE IV in a Day
Learn dBASE Programming in a Day
Learn DOS in a Day
Learn DrawPerfect in a Day
Learn Excel for Windows in a Day
   (Ver. 3.0 & 4.0)
Learn FoxPro 2.0 in a Day
Learn Freelance Graphics for
   Windows in a Day
Learn Generic CADD 6.0 in a Day
Learn Harvard Graphics 3.0 in a Day
Learn Lotus 1-2-3 in a Day
Learn Lotus 1-2-3 Ver. 2.4 in a Day
Learn Microsoft Assembler in a Day
Learn Microsoft Works in a Day
Learn Norton Utilities in a Day
Learn Novell NetWare Software in a
   Day
Learn OS/2 in a Day
Learn Pacioli 2000 Ver. 2.0 in a Day
Learn PageMaker 4.0 in a Day
Learn PAL in a Day
Learn Paradox 4.0 in a Day
Learn Paradox for Windows in a Day
Learn Pascal in Three Days
Learn PC-Paintbrush in a Day
Learn PC-Tools 8.0 in a Day
Learn PlanPerfect in a Day
Learn Q&A in a Day
Learn Quattro Pro 4.0 in a Day

Popular Applications Series Cont.
Learn Quicken in a Day
Learn Turbo Assembler Programming
   in a Day
Learn Ventura 4.0 in a Day
Learn Windows in a Day
Learn Windows NT in a Day
Learn Word 2.0 for Windows in a Day
Learn WordPerfect 5.2 for Windows in
   a Day
Learn WordPerfect in a Day (2nd
   Edition)
Mailing Lists using dBASE
Moving from WordPerfect for DOS to
   WordPerfect for Windows
Object-Oriented Programming using
   Turbo C++
Presentations with Harvard Graphics
Programming Output Drivers using
   Borland C++
WordPerfect Macros
WordPerfect 6.0 Survival Skills
Write Your Own Programming
   Language using C++

At A Glance Series
Ami Pro 3.0 for Windows at a Glance
dBASE IV 2.0 at a Glance
dBASE for Windows at a Glance
Excel 4.0 at a Glance
FoxPro 2.5 at a Glance
FoxPro for Windows at a Glance
Lotus 1-2-3 at a Glance
Lotus 1-2-3 for Windows at a Glance
Microsoft Windows at a Glance
Microsoft Word 5.5 at a Glance
Paradox 4.0 at a Glance
Paradox for Windows at a Glance
Quattro Pro 4.0 at a Glance
Quattro Pro for Windows at a Glance
Windows NT at a Glance
Word 2.0 for Windows at a Glance
WordPerfect 6.0 at a Glance
WordPerfect for Windows 5.2 at a
   Glance

Call Wordware Publishing, Inc. for names of the bookstores in your area
(214) 423-0090

Other Books from Wordware Publishing, Inc.

Computer Aided Drafting
Illustrated AutoCAD (Release 11)
Illustrated AutoCAD (Release 12)
Illustrated AutoLISP
Illustrated AutoSketch 2.0
Illustrated Generic CADD Level 3

Database Management
Illustrated dBASE III Plus
Illustrated dBASE IV 1.1
Illustrated Force 2
Illustrated FoxPro 2.0

Desktop Publishing
The Desktop Studio: Multimedia with
 the Amiga
Illustrated PFS:First Publisher 2.0 &
 3.0
Illustrated PageMaker 4.0
Illustrated Ventura 3.0 (Windows Ed.)
Illustrated Ventura 3.0 (DOS/GEM Ed.)
Illustrated Ventura 4.0

General and Advanced Topics
111 Clipper Functions
The Complete Communications
 Handbook
The Desktop Studio: Multimedia with
 the Amiga
Financial Modeling using Lotus 1-2-3
Graphic User Interface Programming
 with C
Illustrated CorelDRAW! 3.0
Illustrated DacEasy Accounting 4.2
Illustrated Harvard Graphics 3.0
Illustrated Novell NetWare 2.x/3.x
 Software
Integrating TCP/IP into SNA
Learn P-CAD Master Designer 6.0
Novell NetWare: Advanced
 Techniques and Applications
Programming On-line Help with C++
Understanding 3COM Networks

Integrated
Illustrated Enable/OA
Illustrated Framework III
Illustrated Microsoft Works 2.0
Illustrated Q&A 3.0 (2nd Ed.)
Illustrated Q&A 4.0

Programming Languages
Illustrated Borland C++ 3.1
Illustrated C Programming (ANSI)
 (2nd Ed.)
Illustrated Clipper 5.0 (2nd Ed.)
Illustrated QBasic for MS-DOS 5.0
Graphics Programming with Turbo
 Pascal
Illustrated Turbo C++
Illustrated Turbo Debugger 3.0
Illustrated Turbo Pascal 6.0

Spreadsheet
Illustrated Excel 4.0 for Windows
Illustrated Lotus 1-2-3 Rel. 2.2
Illustrated Lotus 1-2-3 Rel. 3.0
Illustrated Quattro

Systems and Operating Guides
Illustrated DR DOS 6.0
Illustrated MS-DOS 5.0
Illustrated UNIX System V
Illustrated Windows 3.1

Word Processing
Illustrated Microsoft Word 5.0 (PC)
Illustrated WordPerfect 1.0 (Macintosh)
Illustrated WordPerfect 5.1
Illustrated WordPerfect for Windows
Illustrated WordStar 6.0
WordPerfect Wizardry: Advanced
 Techniques and Applications

Call Wordware Publishing, Inc. for names of the bookstores in your area
(214) 423-0090